Freaks, Angels, and other Anomalies

It's much easier to tame a fanatic than it is to breathe life into a corpse!

Freaks, Angels, and other Anomalies

Freaks, Angels, and other Anomalies

Inspired by true stories

All copyright laws apply to this document

This book is the sole property of Phillip Bryan Hartsock and Linefork Publishing

Table of Contents

Intro	7
Honey, the Dogs…	11
I Am NOT Snoring!!	21
The Blue Stuff	31
The Stress Test	45
Hope	59
Sarge	69
Pags	89
The McLaury's	101
Lucifer	117
Elijah	131
Stroker	139
Wild Bill	149
You Might Be a Hillbilly If…	157
A Night to Remember!	171
Midnight Run	185
The Last One Picked	197

Reincarnation _____ 209

Virgil Lee _____ 215

Intro

Ever meet someone and, the first time you set eyes on them, you go, "OK, this guy is a couple of sandwiches shy of a picnic!"? You know instinctively that something is <u>seriously</u> wrong with them, *mentally*. Everything they touch is a complete disaster and their disastrous persona rubs off on everyone they come near. Then, there are others who just exude an air that illuminates everything around them. They walk into a room and attention is immediately drawn to them like mosquitoes to a bug light. It's hard to explain sometimes, but, you can just feel it in your bones that God actually put them in that place, and time, solely for your benefit. Meet Hope, the cat who saved my life! We have all heard the cliché, "The Lord works in mysterious ways", throughout our lives. On the contrary, the Lord sometimes works in ways that are painfully obvious, if you know what to look for. Meet the McClaury's.

This book is a combination of "Freaks, Angels, and Anomalies" that I have encountered during my lifetime. Some I have known from childhood, others I met as an adult, and yet others were observed in the abstract. See the Stress Test. I just felt that these people, and circumstances, were just too extraordinary to not tell the whole world about. Take this book, sit back, and perch yourself near the fireplace. If you prefer, pour yourself a cup of coffee or tea, pop open a beer can, or just chew on a bag of chips for a while. Enjoy a long overdue, well-deserved, laugh, or cry, and don't take life too serious or you'll end up like me!

Thanks in advance for your continued support,

Phillip Bryan Hartsock

Freaks, Angels, and other Anomalies

Freaks, Angels, and other Anomalies

Honey, the Dogs...

So, it's three o'clock in the morning, the witching hour, and I'm having a great dream about being on a beach somewhere with a boat drink in my hand, sand all over me, hot women scantily clad in their tiny bikini's dot the beach here and there, the waves caressing my brain like a waterfall..., and...; what the hell is that? Sounds like a bell! Why would a bell be ringing on the beach? Maybe a lifeguard's dinner bell? Ow, the lifeguard just jabbed me in the ribs with his umbrella pole causing sharp stabbing pains to run through my ribcage, and is now yelling for me to wake up. No wait, that's a woman's voice, OK, it's a female lifeguard and, hey, I recognize her voice. But dad-gum, *what...* is that... smell? It smells like...*eww...ugh...*

"Phil, wake up! Phil, *wake up*! Phillip, WAAAKE UP!!!"

"Whaaaa...ttt?"

"Max just pooed and jumped down, he needs to go out."

"You have *got* to be kidding me!"

"No, didn't you hear his collar bell?"

"Dog-gone-it, why can't *you* take him out?"

"I took him out *last time*!"

"So, I changed the oil in your car the last time! You gonna change it next time?"

"Quit being a butt-hole and get up and take the dogs out, PLEASE!"

"Honey, it's three degrees out!"

"Oh, so dogs don't go when it's three degrees out? Do *you* go when it's three degrees out?"

"Well no, not outside! Especially not at three o'clock in the morning! Something about the number *three* just doesn't do it for me!"

"Well if you don't get up and take them out you're gonna be cleaning up some number *two*, now get up and take the dogs out and quit being so lazy!"

Somehow, this was not what I envisioned in my future the day we went shoe shopping and came home with a beautiful Golden Retriever we affectionately named Jake. Nor was it my fantasy when we picked up our Yorkshire Terrier, Max. So, knowing I have to work tomorrow morning at six doesn't make this process any easier. I slowly roll out from underneath the warm covers as the dogs turn uneasily in tight little circles at the foot of the bed and stare at me as if to say; "Hey man, can you pick it up a little, I've got a Chalupa goin' on here!"

It takes me at least three to four minutes to get prepped for the trip outdoors into the blizzard-like conditions that are common here in Western Pennsylvania wintertime. I put on my long-johns, my sweatshirt, my sweatpants, my wool socks, and my winter hat. Then I put on my parka, my winter boots, my gloves and wrap my face in a scarf. I look like an astronaut! The dogs are now dancing in unison around my feet and chirping like birds because of the smokey-links poking out their behinds. I reach for the leash as Max starts the *pre-dump* hunker, and gets that seriously strained look on his face. I yell at him and bring him out of his flat-line just long enough to clip the leash onto his collar and scoop him up.

"Honey, did you put Max's little booties on?"

"Not yet dear, *getting' it though*." "Dang-it!" (I mumble under my breath)

Colleen bought these little multi-colored, wool, attachments for Max in order to keep his feet warm. They are tethered to his legs by Velcro straps that you have to put on one at a time while holding him in your lap; the whole time he kicks his legs because he hates them so much. After about two minutes of getting kicked, I finally get through the agony of putting these on and drag him out the door. Jake follows, still chirping, and races toward the pines we have planted along the property line, *his triage*! Freezing rain fell a few days ago on top of the thirteen inches of snow and the back yard looks like Glacier National Park. Jake is stabbing deep holes into the tundra with his long legs as the snow and ice crunch and crack under his weight. Jake has learned that by dancing in tight circles he can wallow out a small round area to poop in without laying his testicles on the ice and has the art of blizzard-pooping mastered for the most part. He takes care of his business, *at least I think*, and heads back towards the house where Colleen is waiting to let him in and give him a treat for being such a nice dog. *Good boy Jake*!

Max is now zig-zagging across the frozen yard trying to find his place and now appears confused. The wind and snow are slowly eating away at my enthusiasm. As we walk, the crunching and crackling of the ice causes Max to pause every time he gets close to conceiving. My teeth are chattering like a jackhammer now as Max starts flipping his booties around as if he's walking on a hot stove. He pulls this trick every time I take him out and it's starting to get old. Not only do I have to make sure he poops, I also have to make sure the booties stay intact because the minute he loses one, that foot comes off the ground and I am now dealing with a frustrated, three-legged dog. Max finally finds a suitable place and starts doing the enhanced circular-expulsion dance in order to extricate his gift into the snow. Just as the deposit is about half-way out, a cave-in occurs and Max disappears below the surface of the ice-cap. Evidently this causes a reverse-the-gears effect on dogs and Max draws the deposit back into the bank, flies up out of the hole, and continues the zig-zagging; now on three legs; a look of panic on his face. Suddenly the wind picks up and starts swirling the snow across the yard in little white tornadoes as Max now decides to drag me back toward the house. I can barely see him now and am slowly losing my vision and my mind. The wind is cutting me to the bone and I feel naked. Just ten minutes ago I was on the beach experiencing nirvana. Two minutes ago Max was giving birth right there in the mud-room and now he wants to drag me back in the house. As self preservation kicks in I start thinking "hmm, I could just *tell her* that he pooped and she wouldn't know the difference." I start easing back toward the house as Max again starts to dart back and forth across the ice looking for another place to go.

"Come on Max, good boy. Let's go get a biscuit! Momma wants to see her good little boy."

As I get closer to the house, the porch light comes on and through the driving snow I see it; my wife's long, boney finger pointing skyward out the crack in the screen door, directing me to turn around and take Max back out into the yard until he poops. I <u>HATE IT</u> when she does *that*! Now I start cussing Max and threatening to leave him outdoors if he doesn't go *quickly*. I pick him up and start squeezing him like a tube of decorative cake-icing. Sensing the urgency, Max gets that look on his face again! Begging him to go in my nicest voice, Max finally decides to give one final push and drops a half a Gherkin on the ice with a clink. Keep in mind I/we have been outside for *at least* ten minutes at this point. Now feeling a sense of accomplishment I head back toward the warm house still carrying Max; visions of sun and waves returning to my head. As soon as I walk in the door, Colleen (Cybil) is waiting with her hands on her hips asking;

"*Where* are his booties?"

I look down and three of the four booties are missing! Somewhere in the back yard they wait for me in icy graves. Now completely frozen to death *and* flabbergasted, I head back out with the flashlight and begin my futile search for these brightly colored little booties. I am *absolutely* seething now, cussing under my breath, my teeth are chattering, my face is a shade of purple I've never seen, and my ears feel like they are going to break and fall off my head! I stab holes in the ice with the large flashlight I carry outdoors. It's a good thing the neighbors can't see me or they would really think I've lost my mind. I search and search and search for another ten minutes and finally find all three booties. I head back toward the house thinking "OK, it's over, back to bed." Who shall I find waiting in the shadows of the mud-room but my lovely wife?

"I think Jake still has to go!"

"WHAT? Have you <u>completely</u> lost your mind?"

"I don't think he finished while ago!"

"Yes he did! *Didn't he?*" *I say squeemishly.*

"'fraid not!"

"He dropped a turban out there! How do you know he has to go again anyway? Did you put a gauge in his behind to see where the poop is?"

"Just take him out on the leash so we don't get woken up again!"

"You mean so *you* don't have to get up and take him out; huh?"

Back out, again, I go onto the glacier with Jake. Jake leads me on a meandering jaunt through the blinding snow again; I feel like Grizzly Adams now and start talking out-loud to myself. I think I'm starting to hallucinate as my brain begins to freeze. I can *barely* feel my face, my hands are numb, I *can't* feel my privates, and I begin wandering aimlessly about the back yard. Jake takes another five minutes to drop out this tiny little malted milk-ball that could have definitely waited until I got up at six. I stumble my way back to the house and almost crawl in the back door. I look in the mirror and there are little balls of frozen snow crusted to my mustache and beard and

I'm as blue as a lobster! After undressing from the three-hundred pounds of clothes I wore outside I finally get back in bed at three-thirty-five. After about ten minutes I'm dozing off and drifting back into my wonderful dream when my lovely wife says;

"Phil, did you lock the back door?"

I shoot straight out of bed and run to the back door so mad I could just kill somebody.

"Good grief woman, couldn't you have asked me that crap while I was still up?"

I think my wife sometimes does this just to torment me for giving her a hard time about getting out of bed. Or, maybe it's just payback for her poor judgment in marrying me. Half an hour later, she starts her dad-burn snoring! "Honey, wake up you're snoring!"

Freaks, Angels, and other Anomalies

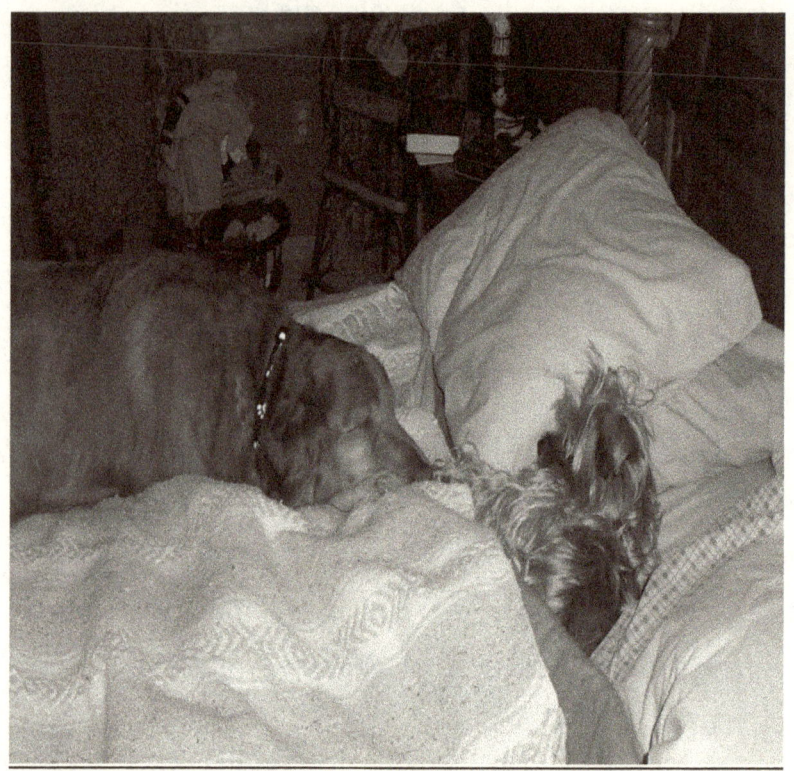

I Am NOT Snoring!!

In any marriage, there are things that cause the best of spouses to argue. I leave the lid off the toothpaste, forget to flush the toilet, leave my clothes laying by the bed, make WAY too many body noises, don't clean up after myself from dinner at times, leave lights on all over the house, and often forget important things my wife may or *may not* have told me the day before. That being said, few things have caused more arguments between my wife and me than snoring. I have no problem *admitting* that I snore and openly agree that I have even awoken myself doing so! My wife, on the other hand, is of the species that cannot, under any circumstance, admit that she snores! Snoring is a genetic trait she received from her father. This man snores so loud that wildlife has ceased to exist within a five-mile radius of their home and her father had to reinforce the windows in order to keep them from shattering. Scientist at the Los

Alamos National Earthquake Laboratory have picked up the tremors and even received a reading of 3.0 on the Richter scale due to his snoring!

I remember the first night we stayed in their home. We had just fallen asleep when I heard the most awful noise coming from somewhere down the hallway. I seriously thought we were being burglarized and threw the covers off myself and prepared to defend us against the intruder;

"Honey, did you hear that?"

"Hear what?"

"HNNNKKKKK, WHBBBBBLLLEEE"

"That!"

"HNNNKKKKK, WH…BBBBBLLLE"

"Oh, that's just Dad!"

"Good grief! How does your Mom sleep through that?"

"Good medication!"

"What the heck does she take, *Morphine*?"

"No, he's been doing that all my life, and probably his too. She just learned to deal with it somehow. Kind of like living near the railroad tracks, you get used to it."

"Do you snore like that too?"

"*Pffft*, NO! I don't snore *at all*."

"Good, I can't sleep with someone who snores."

"Oh, don't worry honey, I don't snore. I promise."

Well, she *wasn't* lying. She really *thinks* she doesn't snore. I thought she didn't either until allergy season came along that first year. At first the snoring wasn't really snoring, it was more of a popping sound kind of like this; *wheeze..., n..tock, wheeze..., n..tock.* I would nudge her and say; *"Honey you're popping, would you please roll over?"* Evidently as we grow older something happens to our breathing apparatus. This popping evolved into another sound sort of like this; *pu...feewwww, pu...fewww, pu...fewww.* These were minor annoyances that I could live with because I was still young and slept quite well. When I was younger I could lie on the beach and sleep through a hurricane and never even stir. As I have gotten older however, I work different shifts and my sleep patterns are usually a wreck, so even the slightest noise wakes me out of a dead sleep. That doesn't remove the fact that my beautiful wife snores like a bear with a stuffy nose. This is a typical dialogue between her and me on any given night;

"*HNNNNNNNNKKKKKKKKKKK,...NNNKK..., pu...fewwww*"

"Honey, roll over you're snoring!"

"No I'm NOT, you're full of it!"

"Oh, so you think I just decided to wake you up and lie to you huh?"

"You're a butthole!" She says as she yanks the covers over her head.

"Why are you calling ME a butthole? *You* were the one snoring!"

"I was NOT snoring!"

"Oh my Gosh! Yes you were!"

"I've been laying here wide awake for the last half-an-hour! Now, please tell me *how in the heck* I can be awake and snore at the same time?"

"The same way your father snored all the pictures off the wall when we were staying at your parents! Remember, your Mom told him HE was snoring too and he argued the point!"

"Phillip, if you don't want to sleep with me, just say so!"

"Honey, if I didn't want to sleep with you don't you think I could be a little more creative than coming up with a bullshit excuse like you snoring?"

"No! *You're an idiot!*"

"Gee thanks."

"Would you just go to sleep!"

"Let me go out to the garage and bring the chainsaw to bed with me. As soon as you go to sleep I'll crank it up and run it wide-open in your ear; how's that?"

"You *really are* a butthole!"

"I'm going to the couch!"

"Good, that's where you wanted to sleep *anyway*. *God forbid* <u>anybody</u> touch you or snore a little bit when *you're* sleeping!"

I have worn out three couches, woken up with knots in my back, and walked crooked for several days a week for the last ten years due to my wife's incessant snoring. We have tried the Breathe-right strips, the Nettie pots, the allergy and sinus medication, and group therapy; nothing has worked. Well, almost nothing.

I grew tired of wasting hard-earned money on all the store-bought remedies so, over the past few years, I developed a system that seems to work quite well depending on the circumstances; i.e., *the spouse must be asleep and snoring*! This patented system is made up of certain moves in the bed and a thesaurus of new words and sounds that stop the snoring just long enough for the victim to go to sleep first. Moves and sounds/words are listed separately here so experiment with each one for a while because all of these may or may not work on *your* spouse.

The "Snore no More" patented routine!

Body moves and other recommendations;

The flip: Grab the covers, wrap them *tightly* around your fist, raise the covers high with your elbow, and yank with all your might. This results in a violent flipping of the spouse's immediate body position into a new position and momentarily wakes her up. The beauty of this move is that by the time she lands back in the bed, you are wrapped tightly in your covers and give off the impression that you are actually sleeping.

The flop: Flop around in bed long enough to wake your spouse and stop the snoring; usually four or five flops will do the trick. Breathing heavily while doing this seems to help too!

The exaggerated pillow-fluff : Roll out of bed *slowly*, make sure to leave the covers pulled back for quick re-entry into the bed, raise the pillow high over your head, slam it down <u>hard</u>, jump back under the covers! Pretend you are now asleep!

The nudge: a slight touch to the calf of your spouse's leg with your heel or big toe.

The knee: Grinding of the sharp point of one's knee (just below the kneecap) into the spouse's quadriceps. (Pressure-point technique)

The bump: a light rubbing of your thumb on her butt. This often causes the <u>*wife*</u> to think you want sex and makes them angry. **Angry = can't sleep = snoring stops**! If you get sex, it's a bonus! *Sorry ladies, this won't work for you*! You touch us with anything in bed and it's on!

The Jab: Poke two fingers firmly into the spouses nostrils, remove quickly so as not to be detected. *Deny everything*!

The hydraulic toe-pinch: Pinching an area of the wife's leg using your big toe and your second toe. (*A technique I learned from my older sister at an early* *age*.) This usually results in a yelp from the spouse. **Wife yelps = dog barks = can't sleep = no more snoring**!

The elbow grind: A slow grinding of the elbow into the spouses ribcage or back. Be sure to release the elbow once you detect movement from the spouse or you <u>could</u> end up getting punched in the head!

Sounds and words that one can use to effectively stop the spouse from snoring;

Chirping bird: Irritating as hell. Not recommended for use in winter months unless you have pet birds.

Growling dog: Be prepared to get up and look out the window for would-be burglars.

Fluttering wings: This sound has been known to cause hallucinations in women. The wife may wake up screaming and flailing her arms in an effort to ward off an invisible attacking bat. <u>Not</u> recommended for anyone with a heart condition!

Race-car sound: This can be blamed on a passing motorist if you live near a highway or city street.

The fake snore: Get as close as possible to spouse's ear, give one good "HNNNNK" and wait. Give a second blast if the first one isn't effective. This usually results in the spouse accusing <u>you</u> of snoring, makes her angry, and now she can't sleep either! *Very gratifying! Again, deny any wrongdoing!*

The whistling bomb-drop: Use only in small increments until the desired affect is achieved.

The simulated mongo-fart: Re-mastered version of the longest fart you've ever ripped. Best when used in conjunction with bad-breath!

Words or combinations of words include:

Hi-jee-beeble: Not really a word but causes light stirring

Heww-unnn, Rollin, Rollin, Rollin, I've got friends in low places, that's a Big One, and OH YEAH...

These words or simulated words leave the impression that you are talking and/or singing in your sleep. The wife may accuse you of having a bad dream when using any combination of these words. Most effective when used with **The Flip or the Flop!**

Did you hear that: This must be used simultaneously with **the elbow Grind** , or **the knee.** This redirects the brain to think of fear and not of pain.

What was that? You mean to tell me you didn't hear that? Most effective when used immediately after **Growling dog** or **Fluttering bird**. Same effect as "**Did you hear that?**"

Oww, stop kicking me! Recommend using this with **The Flip.** After the wife's body falls back onto the bed in the new position, you accuse *her* of kicking *you* while having a nightmare!

Although all of these don't work all the time, they have proven effective in my experience and have improved my quality of sleep many times over. When using any of these either by themselves or in combination, I can promise you that your spouse will stop snoring long enough for you to go to sleep before her. If none of these works for you, then *you* are the one snoring and you should probably go sleep on the couch!

The Blue Stuff

Having three kids to keep entertained was becoming difficult for my wife and I so we decided to sell our classic car and buy a camper. We searched, and searched, for just the right camper, in just the right place, and finally agreed on a camper that was already set up in a beautiful island campground, Kibbe's Island. Kibbe's Island sits right on the pristine Allegheny River just south of Tionesta, Pennsylvania. Having loads of experience in primitive camping, I thought I knew just about everything about the subject. Modern camping would be a breeze. We had a beautiful lot, everything indoors, real beds, a kitchen, running water, a stove, microwave oven, inboard stereo system, a toilet and shower! What could possibly be hard about this? Heck, we even had a covered front porch! How could anyone possibly ask for more? This is great, we thought!

Our 1986 Holiday Rambler had a few cobwebs we had to work out though, *real cobwebs*, in the furnace and hot-water heater. It gets a little chilly at night in the spring here so we decided to light the two in order to enjoy the full amenities offered by modern camping. While nearly burning my face off trying to light the hot-water heater, I noticed our elderly neighbor lighting his heater and decided I should probably ask for help before I flash-fried myself. I walked over and introduced myself, and quickly realized that my neighbor was very hard of hearing. I figured this out quick because he shouts everything so he can hear himself;

"Hello sir, my name is Phil" (I extended my hand)

> "Jill, what kind of name is that for a feller to have?"

"Wha..., oh no, sir, I said Phil."

> "Oh, Bill. Well that's more like it! What can I do for you young man?"

"No, *not Bill*. Phil!"

> "Well, what do you want to feel, Bill?"

"No sir, MY NAME IS PHIL!" (Now shouting)

"How's 'at? I'm a little hard of hearing outta that ear?"

"OH, THAT"S OK SIR, I'LL JUST TALK LOUDER! MY NAME IS... P-H-I-L, PHIL!"

"What can I do for you?"

"I need some help getting my water heater lit."

"We don't have water meters in the campground, you just pay one fee for water and it's the same for everybody!"

"NO, I need my WATER HEATER LIT!"

"Oh, well why you didn't just say that, you don't have to yell! Names Arthur, my friends call me Art."

"OK ART. NICE TO MEET YOU." I yell.

After getting over the speech hurdle, Art really turned into an asset and showed me the ins and outs of modern day camping. I helped him out around his camper stacking wood, and often would check on his place or mow his lawn when he was away. Art also advised me of all the fees associated with camping including the sewer fee. My wife is not one to throw away money needlessly. So, she decided that I should just take care of the sewer myself, and avoid paying the thirty-five dollar annual fee. For some reason I just presumed that this only involved turning a handle and letting the sewer into the underground holding tank.

I WAS WRONNNNG!!!

One summer weekend, we invited several family members to come to camp with us. We all brought lots of food, plenty of adult beverages, and had a great time. After eating five-hundred pounds of food, everybody had to use the bathroom several times that day. We all blamed it on a batch of chili that we felt had given everybody stomach problems. I'll bet you we went through five or six rolls of toilet paper that day too! By evening time, all of the family had gone home and we were settling in for the night. Colleen always makes the kids use the restroom before they go to bed so they're not up all hours of the night clanging and banging around. My son says;

"Mommy, the toilet won't flush."

"You have to hold down on the handle honey."

"I am Mommy but my poop is spinning around and the water is getting high in the bowl."

"Phillip, put your beer down and come look at the toilet."

"Honey, I just built this nice fire, can't it wait?"

"No, it can't, it's stinking up the camper!"

"That's probably just from him pooping, give it a minute."

"No, it's because there's ten turds in here dancing around in the toilet bowl calling your name."

I don't know how, *or why*, but my kids have the largest turds I've ever seen. You could build cabins with these things I swear! One of them will fill a toilet bowl by itself. Not only are they the biggest, they are also the most pungent! Imagine ten-thousand skunks spraying all at the same time inside an eight by ten bathroom and you might get the picture; *maybe*! Camper bathrooms are even smaller than eight by ten; ours was about three by three not counting the shower. Whoever invented these torture chambers should be sentenced to ten years of solitary confinement in one! I put my beer down, walk in the camper, and find my son poking at his poop with the toilet brush. I run him out of the bathroom and try to ascertain the problem. Yep, definitely plugged up. I grab the plunger and go to work on the clog for a few minutes. This does nothing but churn everything into a big stinking bowl of goulash. Ready to give up, I go back outside and finish my beer next to the fire. Colleen says,

"Phillip, why don't you go ask Art for help?"

"At this hour?"

"Well, you can't just leave the stuff sit here all night!"

"Sure we can, just close the lid!"

"I swear you wouldn't breathe unless you had to!"

"That would be convenient about now!"

"Go get Art!"

Pissed off over the whole idea of exchanging my nightcap by the fire for cleaning poop out of the toilet, I walk next door and knock. I can see through the window that Art is fast asleep in his chair with the newspaper across his lap. The TV is blaring so loud I could hear it before I walked up on the porch. At first I knock the way I would anywhere else, a light rap. That doesn't work so I knock harder the next time. No luck! I pound on the door with my fist, this time hard. Art stirs for a minute, then dozes right back off. I give up at this point and go back to the camper where my angry wife awaits.

"Where's Art."

"Sleeping."

"Wake him up!"

"That's rude."

"Sleeping in a cesspool is *more* rude! Now go wake him up!"

"He has a shotgun lying across his lap!"

"Good, maybe he'll shoot you!"

"Yeah, maybe he will and I won't have to clean out the poop tank!"

Realizing she isn't going to take no for an answer, I walk out of the camper mad as hell. I walk over and start rocking the camper, pounding on the door, and yelling; "HEY ART, HEY ART!" Art wakes up now and comes to the door.

"What can I do for you young feller?"

"Hey man, my commode is clogged and I can't get it to open."

"The road ain't closed; I just came through there today; why is it closed anyway?"

"NO. I SAID MY COMMODE IS CLOGGED!"

"Oh, I see. Give me a minute. Let me put some old clothes on."

Art heads towards his bedroom and emerges ten minutes later carrying a circular, spring-like, piece of equipment with a handle attached to one end.

"This ought to do the trick."

"What is that?"

"A snake."

"What's it for?"

"It helps unclog toilets. See here, you just open your commode lid, put this in one end, turn it with the handle, and walaa, out comes the poopies!"

"ART I THINK IT'S JUST TOO FULL FROM ALL THE PEOPLE USING IT TODAY."

"Well, in that case, we gotta empty it."

"EMPTY WHAT?"

"The holding tank with the blue stuff in it."

"BLUE STUFF?"

"Yeah, the stuff you put in the holding tank to keep the poop from smelling so bad."

"OH, OK. MAKES SENSE I GUESS."

Art brings his flashlight, points under the camper, and yells;

"Reach under there and pull that blue thing out with the wheels on it."

This is the first time I've seen this contraption but it looks like a big blue gas can that sits real low to the ground with two wheels on one end. On the end opposite the wheels is a twist-off lid where the sewer is supposed to go, I presume. On the other end is a plug that, when opened, allows the air inside the container to escape as the tank fills. Art yells;

"Now I'm gonna hook this here hose up to this tank. When we get everything hooked up, I'll pull the relief valve and let the sewer run into the tank. You hold on to the tank and tell me when it gets full and I'll close the relief valve, OK?"

"OK!"

"Don't forget that you have to leave the other end open so the air inside the tank can escape. OK?"

"I GOT IT, ART!"

We hook everything up and make sure it's all tight so as not to spill any sewer on the ground. Art and I ready ourselves at our positions and Art says;

"OK, ready?"

"YES ART, I'M READY."

I hear a gurgling sound, a rush of water and debris, and the hissing sound of air leaking from the caddy tank I am now holding. Suddenly, the most God-awful smell hits me in the face and I recoil. Then, my end of the tank starts gushing sewer. Poop and toilet paper are running all over the ground, on my hands, and under the camper.

"ART, SHUT IT OFF! IT'S *FULL*....!"

"NOW you just tell me when it gets full?" *Art said with his back to me.*

"ART, SHUT IT OFF, IT'S RUNNING ALL OVER THE GROUND! *Hew...LL; hew...ll, oit...*"

Art never heard my incoherent moans after that. Now, the gears in my throat are in full reverse and I almost barf. My desperate cries to shut the valve on the holding tank slowly dissipate but it's too late anyway. I'm covered in sewer and, *seriously*, gagging. I can feel my dinner trying to fight its way out of my esophagus and up through my nose. Out the dark window my wife says;

"*Hew...it*, God, *what* is that awful smell?"

"It's Pine-Sol, what the heck do you think it is? *Hew...it...* This could have waited until tomorrow Colleen! *Dad-gummit!*"

I look over and Art now is fighting the hose trying to get it back on my end of the tank as the tank continues to spray raw sewer. I can't get far enough away, and abandon poor Art in his time of need. Colleen yells;

"Get over here and help that poor..., *hew...it....,* man!"

"You help him; this was your bright idea *anyway!*"

Finally Art gets the lever shut off and the small tank closed. He's covered in sewer, mad as heck, and walking in circles trying not to gag. Art eventually just throws his hands up and walks back toward his camper, leaving me all alone with this festering pile of doo-doo. Now, Colleen wants me to clean this mess up!

"You can't just leave it there!"

"Watch me!"

"Phillip, we have to clean this up!"

"We? You mean ME!"

"*Whatever!* You're a butthole!"

"Colleen I'm *seriously* going to puke! I can't possibly do this tonight, I'll try tomorrow!"

"You're an idiot!"

"Now I'm an idiot? Thanks Miss Einstein for coming up with this *brilliant* idea!"

We slept that night with cotton balls crammed and compacted into our noses so far that it took us ten minutes just to dig them out the next morning. Before we could even think about eating breakfast, I knew I had to overcome my weak stomach and clean the hazardous waste site I had created the night before, and drag the small tank to the big dumping station across the campground. I re-stuffed my nose with cotton and made my best effort to overcome the sickening smell of the sewer. Unfortunately the blue stuff doesn't work as well as it is supposed to and penetrates cotton. My first idea was to drag this thing to the dump station by hand. I quickly found out that there was no possible way I would make it to the dump station without barfing so, this idea, I quickly abandoned. My next brain storm was to tie it to the back of the Jeep with a rope and tow it to the station. Great idea! I tied everything up real nice, got in the Jeep, and towed my load slowly across the island toward the dump-station. For some reason, everyone was glaring at me as I crept along with my volatile load, maybe they're just jealous of this grand idea I came up with. Upon arrival to the dump-station, I quickly realized why everyone was glaring at me. There was a row of mushy turds lying in scattered parts along the campground road, I mean they were everywhere. Evidently they had sloshed and slopped right out of the container as I hit the bumps and mud-holes in the road; leaving a trail of deathly odor in their wake. By the time I reached the dump station, I only had about a gallon of waste in the container to dump. Now, I had to go back, grab a shovel and a dust pan, and sweep all those damn turds back up! By the time I got back to the camper I was turning shades of Magenta and Lime green and ready to puke. I walked into the camper where Colleen and her best friend Brenda were fixing breakfast;

"Get out of here, you smell horrible!"

"Please honey, I'm gonna puke! *Hew...it...*"

"No way, get the hell out of here, you're gonna ruin our breakfast!"

There have been only a few times in life where I felt like crying and begging to my wife. This was *definitely* one of them! I glared at her through tears as if to say "Please honey, I'm dying here!" Sensing my desperation, she relented and let me wash my hands in the kitchen sink and take a shower. I had a nightmare that night about being flushed down a camper toilet and woke up with the cold sweats. As soon as I got out of bed the next morning, I went straight to the campground shack, and paid my thirty-five dollar annual sewer fee to Lester, the campground owner. To date, the best investment I've ever made!

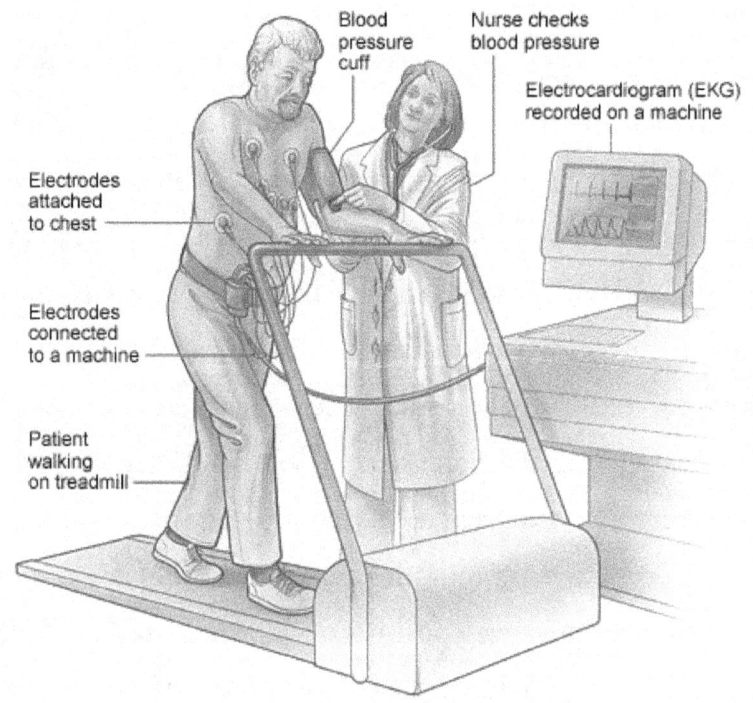

The Stress Test

Modern medicine, as we know it, has advanced in light years since the first time I can remember going into a hospital. Thanks to the advancement of such things as nuclear medicine, doctors and scientist can now successfully perform heart transplants at the rate of production of a Volkswagen. The technology now exists to do liver transplants, face reconstruction, kidney transplants, and many other surgeries designed to improve the quality of life. Doctors have successfully put boobs on a man, and testicles on a woman, and somehow made them work. Or, at least, leave the appearance that they work. Granted, that's enough to make you scratch your head. But, what bothers me even more is this; it appears that there are some major scams, designed by the medical world, to squeeze every penny they can out of insurance companies, through a series of diabolical tests. The catch is, half of the time, these tests aren't even recommended if you don't carry good health insurance. Moreover, if you reach a certain age, there are mandatory experiments designed into the scam as scare tactics, to scare you into taking these tests. But again; *only* if you have good insurance. If you walk into a doctor's office, look even remotely unhealthy, and pull out an insurance card, here's what will happen. Every orifice on your body is gonna get poked, prodded, and manipulated, until they find something, *or make something*, wrong with you! And, you are definitely going to have to subject yourself to some bizarre, unnecessary, tests!

Ok, for those of you who have been healthy all of your lives; go jump off a bridge, now! You may as well prime yourselves for the future. I was healthy all of my life, too, until I reached forty. Then, things started breaking left and right, I can't walk straight, and I get sick a lot more than I used to. Heck, I threw my back out one day just from sneezing too hard! I knew I was getting old but didn't realize how fragile I really was. Another time, I was out in the back yard playing badminton with my three teenagers. My son, being the best athlete in the family, sent this beauty of a serve right into the back corner of my area. I had been in this situation many times before, and thought nothing of it. What I hadn't taken into consideration at the time was this; the ground was wet, I had no shoes on, I was forty years old, they were teenagers! I charged, my plant-foot slipped, my back surged forward without the rest of my body, and I hit the ground, HARD! I slowly pulled myself off the ground and tried to play on as if nothing had happened. After that, every time I tried to go after the birdie, my brain would say go get the nice little birdie, you can do it! My body, however, wouldn't cooperate, and just stood there swarping the racket around in the air like an old woman trying to swat fly's. I became really concerned, and eventually went to several doctors, before finding out I had a severely pinched nerve from a slipped disc in my lower back. I was recommended for physical therapy which helped to some degree, but, not as much as I had hoped. I still have to deal with the pain on a regular basis and hope I never have to have surgery. Especially if it's anything like a stress test!

Several years earlier, I was introduced to this battery of tests after waking in the middle of the night with chest discomfort. Here's how it went down. One morning, my best friend and I had been lifting weights. I had the most weight I have ever lifted on the bench press, over three-hundred pounds. I would never attempt anything heavy without a spotter. However, a spotter does you no good when you growl at him, and threaten him, if he gets anywhere near the bar. Being stubborn, I wanted to exceed my best lift by ten pounds that day, and had the weight half-way to the rack when I stalled. My ass came up off the bench, my spine went toward the ceiling, my left shoulder dropped, the weight bar dipped to one side, and I stubbornly fought the weight off for about fifteen seconds. I must have looked like a praying Mantas lying on its back and trying to flip itself over. Finally, realizing I wouldn't be able to push through, I called on my spotter. Together, we returned the weight to the rack, and finished our routine for the day. That night I experienced serious chest discomfort and thought I may be having a heart attack. The next morning, I advised my wife that I should probably go to the hospital and get myself checked. Upon reporting to the Emergency Room (E.R.), I was subjected to a litany of tests. I got the MRI, the brain scan, the EKG, and the CT scan. I got it all. Except, that is, for the stress test. Whoever the mental giant was that invented this should be taken out and shot! Or, better yet, should have to take the test himself, in the same manner and circumstance as I, every day, for a month straight! My doctor, I won't mention his name here, scheduled me for this space aged, battery of lab experiments designed for Gerbils. His sales pitch was this; Sir, the only way I can tell you <u>for sure</u> that nothing is wrong with your heart, is by doing a series of tests. This scared the crap out of me because I've had cousins die in their sleep due to the fact that they were too reluctant to go see a doctor.

So, I agreed to have the tests. I was advised to not eat or drink anything after midnight, and, to be at the hospital at 0500 hours the following day. "We really shouldn't postpone this" he said. No big deal, I thought, as I had been through this part of the routine before because of a previous, minor, outpatient surgery. I arose at 0400 hours, took my shower, brushed my teeth, and faithfully reported to the hospital window to register like everyone else does, like a good little robot. *Yabba, Dabba, Flippin, DO!!!* As I approached the window, off to my left, I could see a room full of elderly people. All of them looked like mental patients! I wondered, "What the heck are they doing up so early?" After all, it wasn't yet five o'clock in the morning. I presented my paperwork, registered, and was directed to have a seat. "Where?" I asked. "Over there!" replied Nurse Krakow, pointing toward the room full of psycho's. I scratched my head, looked around for a room full of younger people, saw none, and entered the psych-ward. The minute I walked in, all eyes turned on me, glaring, staring, and eyeballing me up and down. There must have been fifteen people in the room, all of them over seventy-five, all tired, and all sleepy. Then the complaining started, slowly at first,

"This is a bunch of crap!" said an elderly man.

> "Oh shut up, we've heard enough of you already!" responded an elderly woman

"Well I ain't had my coffee this mornin'"

> "So what butt-hole, *neither* has anyone else!"

"It's bad enough I gotta get up at three-thirty! Now I can't have my coffee, I can't smoke in here, my stomach's a-growlin', my butt hurts, and I gotta be stuck in a room with you!"

"Oh, well excuse me, *Mr. Perfect*! What makes you think *any of us* are happy to be here? I couldn't sleep last night because my husband snored and farted all night. The dog is half deaf so he barks every time my husband farts or snores! Then, the cat puked on my pillow, and I ended up on the couch! All of that, just so I could get up at three o'clock, take a bath, do my hair, clean my teeth, get dressed, call my sister to come and get me, and now this! I'm stuck in a room with your old, cantankerous, ass!"

"I'll bet your old man's happy, ai*n't he?*"

On and on they went for several minutes, back and forth, back and forth! Then, all of the other old men and women started bickering, and I thought I was gonna be caught in a riot. I began to wonder if this wasn't part of the stress test. For the next hour, one by one, the crowd dwindled. Finally, my name was called, and I was led out of the room by a very rude, older nurse, Hilda. She must have been seventy years old, smelled like a wet ashtray and a beer keg, and barked orders as if I were a new recruit in *her* boot camp! After being led into a room full of treadmills, I was strapped to a-hundred different electrical leads, an oxygen mask, hooked to a tether designed to keep me from falling, and directed to climb onto a vacant treadmill. All around me were older people, huffing, puffing, and cussing, laboring away at their orders, as directed by Nurse Hilda. Then came my orders,

"OK sonny, here's what we're gonna do. We're gonna start you out real nice and slow. Then, we're gonna speed it up a little, increase the incline, work you up a good heart rate, shoot some dye in you, and get some numbers for the doctor. OK?"

"Yes ma'am."

"OK, here we go."

Nurse Hilda pressed a few buttons on the machine, glared at me, and walked away. As I walked, I thought, what would happen if something serious were wrong with me? What would my wife do? How would she make ends meet? I immediately began to stress. Then, the sight of all the wires hanging loosely from my body, bouncing along with the rhythm of my gait, began to bother me. I felt like a Guinea Pig. I could just picture a bunch of short little doctors all dressed in white, wearing glasses, and holding vials, standing around behind a one way glass in the next room planning my surgery. Would it be a triple bypass, open heart, stints? Who knew? This stressed me out even more. I momentarily forgot about all the leads hanging from me, and settled into my thoughts, trying not to stress too much. After all, I wanted to pass this test so I could get on with my life without worrying if I were going to check out any time soon.

After a few minutes, the nurse returned to increase the speed, as well as the incline, of my machine. As the whirring sound of the motor increased with speed, I noticed all of the numbers on the machine climbing, as the colorful lights flashed away. My heart rate, blood pressure, and emotions began to increase as well. The leads began to flop around a little more now, and probably gave off the impression of a giant, *running*, bowl of Linguini. My breathing became a little more labored as my legs and back began to feel the pressure. A few more minutes passed and my lungs began to swell. Here comes Nurse Hilda, *again*, to up the ante, now smiling as she set the new parameters of the machine.

"Hang on dear, now comes the hard part."

"I thought this *was* the hard part!"

"Oh no, not yet. It gets MUCH harder!"

The machine was really kicking now, the motor sounding like a washing machine on the spin cycle. After a minute or so, I *really* started huffing and puffing, sweating profusely, legs aching, lungs swollen up like blimps, and wires flopping all over the place. My head was now way out in front of the rest of my body; my arms began to flail like I was running down into a ravine. The sweat began pouring off me like water from a pitcher. I have always been duck-footed and slower than a snail! The toes of my feet are now on the very back edge of the screaming treadmill, my nose is touching the cross-bar, I am losing oxygen, and the numbers on the machine are now off the charts. Here comes the nurse again, cranking up the heat!

"Let me know when you feel winded." She says with a giggle.

Here I am running wide open, *uphill*, almost lying on my stomach, sweating my butt off, barely breathing, and this woman can't tell I'm winded? I could have sheared her teeth off at the gums. Barely able to speak now, I uttered,

"O.....K...... (huff-huff) NOW!!!"

"Just a minute, we have to shoot some dye in you."

Now, Nurse Hilda speeds the machine up even more, increases the incline, and then, leaves to get her dye injector! After two more minutes, I'm practically dead, and holding on to the cross bar in front of me as if I'm hanging from the bumper of a truck on the Yungas Road. She shoots the dye in me, my heart races out of control, my nerves are racked, all the numbers on the machine are now increasing fast. How in the world is anyone, much less older folks, supposed to pass this sadistic test? Lance Armstrong would be pushing the limits of human capability to pass this one! Then, this witch tells me; "Keep running until I tell you to stop."

"Look, I'm... dying... here! Why... didn't you tell me... before that... I had to... prompt you... when I was ready?"

"I didn't want to stress you out!"

At this point, all of the numbers disappeared, and turned into straight, fluorescent, lines. My mind goes blank. I was so mad that the veins in my head were sticking out like #2 pencils. I almost fell twice, and almost crapped my pants! Finally the puppetmaster let me off the treadmill and returned me to the waiting room. Quite naturally, all of the psycho's had returned by now, and yes, they were seriously complaining,

"I'm hungry!"

"Go eat then, stupid!"

"Who you callin' stupid? Stupid!"

You get the picture, right? An hour later I was called out of the room and advised by the good doctor,

"Son..., I saw a shadow on your heart"

"Well, *nooo*... s#*!, Doctor House! After that lab experiment, it's a darn wonder you didn't see a swollen, bleeding, Granny Smith apple in there!"

"We're gonna have to do a heart catheterization on you."

"What?"

This sounded like certain death to me until he better explained it. Now, I was given the option, again, of not knowing what was wrong with me, or, knowing "for sure", *if* I went through the out-patient surgery. Obviously I wanted to know, so, again I agreed. After a week of fretting and missing work, scared to death that my life may be shorter than I had planned, I found out, as suspected, there was absolutely nothing wrong with my heart! What I had was a partial tear in my rotator cuff. Nothing more! Now, some jack-ass wanted to perform shoulder surgery on me! This doctor told me that I needed immediate surgery to correct this tear. I said, "Forget it; I'll deal with the pain". I quit lifting heavy after that and eventually the pain dissipated. I haven't had any problems since. That year, five other people in my place of employment, *all with good health insurance*, were subjected to the same battery of tests, by the same doctor! Guess what? Nothing was found to be wrong with their hearts either! I'll bet if I would have walked into his office *without insurance*, with my jugular sliced and pumping like a blown oil well; he would have wrapped my neck in duct tape, and sent me packing!

    The home-run I got out of all this is simple. If you have insurance, prepare yourself for unnecessary surgery. You're gonna get it whether you need it or not! In my uneducated, unprofessional, biased opinion, this is the real reason we have a health care crisis in our country. There's just too much easy money to be harvested by doctors, from insurance companies, for them to pass up. I'm not saying that all doctors are unscrupulous. However, many of them are, and unless I've dealt with them for many years, I just don't trust them anymore. Basically unless I'm dead or dying, I don't go to the doctor! My buddy Pags summed it up from his perspective one day after his wife suggested he get a colonoscopy,

"You mean to tell me they can put big hooters on a man, testicles on a woman, fly a space ship around the earth at 18,000 miles an hour and tell you to the millisecond when and where it's gonna land, but they still gotta shove their finger up your behind to tell you if you have pollops? Well, I ain't buying it man!"

End of story!

Hope

There are times in life when we all feel like we have hit the end of our rope and nothing really seems to matter anymore. Nor does it seem worthy of the struggle we have to go through to achieve that which we seek in everyday life. Although I was doing well in life, at the age of thirty-five I hit a brick wall, and for some reason couldn't pull myself out of a downward spiral. I have always thought of myself as mentally tough and most of my peers would agree. "Depression", as defined by medicine.net, is "An illness that involves the body, mood, and thoughts, that affects the way a person eats and sleeps, the way one feels about oneself, and the way one thinks about things". If you have ever suffered from depression I'm sure you understand the definition fully. If you haven't suffered from the illness yet; give it time, you definitely will, that is, provided you live long enough.

A chain of events led to my bout with depression and it soon became clear that I was in trouble and needed help. The year was Two-Thousand and One and it started out with a bang. In February I was assaulted by a mentally challenged inmate and as I was in the emergency room at the hospital, a news flash came on that my favorite race car driver, Dale Earnhardt, wrecked in turn four while blocking for his teammates on the last lap of the Daytona Five-Hundred; he later died as a result of blunt force trauma to the head and chest. Two months later, several of my long-time co-workers were fired for impropriety with inmates! Then, on September, 11, terrorist's hijacked four jumbo jets and committed mass murder in the worst ever attack of this scale on American soil. Like most of America, I was enraged at this cowardly act and had no way to retaliate. Things just kept getting worse as the year wore on and to add to the mess, my bank allowed our account to be emptied to the tune of fourteen-hundred dollars by some unscrupulous attorney who had garnished my account due to an automobile loan I had forfeited on ten years prior. Things only got worse from there, our beloved Yorkshire terrier, Max, gave in to cancer two weeks before Christmas. Just for good measure, while working the block the day after Christmas, as I sat at a steel table filling out my paperwork on all of the inmates who were on a suicide watch; I tried to sneak a fart out and accidentally crapped my pants! I was in a rut that seemingly there was no way out of.

Being a corrections officer is stressful enough. Add to that, the fact that I was not getting the proper amount of sleep, wasn't eating the right foods, my wife was sick and in need of major surgery and, well, *you get the picture*! There were times that I would suffer both ends of the emotional polar where one minute I'd be mad for no reason at all, the next minute, very sad and ready to just break down and cry! Although I was never to the point of being suicidal, I was definitely suffering from major depression.

I had been taught, or programmed, by my father not to show any signs of weakness as this was looked down upon by most of his and, later, my peers. As a result I stuffed everything in front of my wife and family and tried to never let it show. I always felt that I was the one who had to be strong for everyone. Depression finally took its toll on me though and I got to the point where I needed help. I let my wife know and she suggested that I pray about it. So, I hit my knees, turned to the most honorable God, and asked Him for help. I asked that He show me some kind of sign, to let me know that I would be OK, and that He would pull me through all of this, to please just give me a small ray of hope!

On New Year's Eve, Colleen and I were taking down Christmas lights from the gutter over the front porch, and were down to the last strand. It was raining that day as I recall, and as I was taking down the ladder to put it away, I heard a very faint *"meow"* coming from somewhere in the distance. I listened intently but couldn't tell where the sound was coming from. I held a finger to my nose in order to get Colleen to pause and listen for a moment.

"Honey, did you hear that?"

"No, what?"

"*Shhh…*, listen."

"*Meeeoowww*" (a little louder this time)

"It sounds like a kitten."

"Who would put a little kitten out in this kind of weather?"

"Maybe it wandered away from the farm?"

"Where is the meow coming from? *Kitty, kitty kitty, here kitty, kitty, kitty.*"

MEEE…OOWWW   (a little louder this time)

"Keep doing that, I think it's across the road in the bushes."

Colleen kept calling the cat as we both walked closer to the sound. We live out in the country on a road between two towns. The sound was obviously coming from across the road and we didn't want the cat trying to cross the road and chance getting ran over. So we walked together toward the sound and, as we got closer, realized that the sound was coming from the other side of two barbed-wire fences. The farmer next door had these in place to keep his livestock contained. I climbed both fences and Colleen kept calling for the kitten. As I crawled on my hands and knees into a thicket of sharp jaggers, the rain started coming down in sheets. As I edged closer to the sound I saw a tiny kitten entrapped, its legs twisted around in one of the jagged bushes. I started talking to the little animal and it responded every time I said anything with a sad little *"meow"*. I reached in and gently untangled its legs and pulled out the cutest little girl kitten I have ever seen. She was gray with black stripes, and had these huge green saucer eyes, and the prettiest little face you've ever seen. She was shivering really bad, soaking wet, and caked with mud and briars; her little ribs showing from days of starvation. Who knows how long the poor thing had been there but she was very glad to see me to say the least. I tucked her gently under my coat to warm her and began talking to her, assuring her that everything was going to be OK now and that her little worries were over. I could feel her little heart beating against mine as I was holding her close to my body to warm her up. I felt like I had rescued an orphan child who had gotten lost in the wilderness. As I climbed back through the two fences, she began massaging my heart with her little paws and I could feel her roll over onto her back as a child does when you hold it, cradled with my arm underneath her. I opened my coat to show Colleen and of course she was almost in tears just looking at the sight of me standing there in the pouring rain holding this wet, starving, little kitten. As we walked closer to the house I said to Colleen;

"Maybe we should keep her?"

"Oh, I don't know, we already have one cat, I'm not sure we need another."

My coat was still open when Colleen said this and the kitten must have surely heard. She stood up on her hind legs and poked her little head out of my coat, placed both of her little paws on either side of my face, and rubbed her little wet nose right on the end of my nose. I was so touched that my eyes welled up with tears and I said to Colleen;

"We are definitely *keeping* this kitten now."

Colleen being the soft hearted person that she is, especially with animals, didn't put up any resistance after that. We took her inside, fed her some warm milk and fresh cat food, gave her a good bath, and coddled over her for the evening. We woke up the next morning and she was lying in the bed between us sleeping like a baby; the softest purr coming from her tiny mouth. As I started stroking her little body she woke up and placed her little paws on my face again like she had the day before.

Over the remainder of winter, the kitten became the center of my attention and cuddled in my arms every day. She caressed my heart, purred in my ear, and followed me everywhere I went. I'm serious, if I stopped she was at my feet rubbing herself off the bottom of my legs and wouldn't be quiet until I picked her up. Also, every day I came home from work she would be waiting on the window sill or the counter purring and dancing around like a little girl waiting for Daddy to come home. Evidently the bad experience of being cold, hungry, and wet, had lasted. The memory of me rescuing her must have elevated me to

Superman status in her feline mind. I was always quick to pick her up too and she continued her cute antics of caressing my face, caressing my heart, and fussing over me every day when I came home from work.

Colleen and I had tossed several names around and could never agree on one. One night in the spring just before bedtime I was praying and recalled the request that I had placed with God. I recalled vividly asking Him to give me some kind of hope so I could pull out of the dive I was in. That's when it hit me like a bolt of lightning that I had found "Hope". I shook Colleen and said:

"Honey, *meet Hope.*"

"What? Why *Hope?*"

"You remember when I was depressed for a while?

"Yeah, why?"

"Have you noticed that I haven't been depressed lately?"

"Not really, but if you say so."

"I prayed the night before we rescued this cat and asked God to send me a sign that I was going to be OK, to give me some kind of hope. Well, here she is, meet *Hope!*"

What I didn't realize at the time was that God put Hope there in the bushes, starving and barely clinging to life, entangled in a mess and no chance of making it without help, *just for me to rescue.* <u>I was that kitten</u> in the bushes and God choreographed the whole episode in order to rescue *me* from my bout with depression. It's Two-Thousand and Ten now and Hope is still alive and doing well. She is the sweetest, and laziest, animal I have ever seen! She cuddles in my lap daily and purrs with ecstasy upon seeing me. Talk about divine intervention!

Animals bring out the best in people. Even the most violent mobster usually has a pet that captivates them and brings out the softer side. There have been adopt-a-pet programs for the most violent inmates in the world that have been successful because of the joy the animals bring to their lives. Hope is definitely one of God's personal Angels and I hope she lives forever, as I am not prepared to lose her anytime soon, or ever! If you have never adapted a pet from a shelter, you owe it to yourself to do, just once!

Sarge

I have encountered many unusual people in life but few have had the affect of warping my brain like the one I am about to introduce you to here. *Sarge*, so nick-named after being dishonorably discharged from the Army for falling asleep *during munitions drills,* outranks anyone I've ever met or known on the bizarre scale! Seriously folks, how in the *hell* do you sleep when bombs are going off all around you? Please allow me to digress.

Sarge is from Arkansas, smokes dope *and* cigarettes, chews *and* dips, pops pills, drinks anything with alcohol content, and eats any organic material that anyone *claims* will tickle the neurotransmitters in his hollow skull. Sarge only has about four good teeth and the few black ones that cling to his brown gums are chipped, broken, or rotten. Sarge's breath smells like a dead groundhog and has been known to wilt flowers and peel the bark right off an Oak tree. Sarge is never one to primp either. His hair looks like he washed it in used motor oil. He has the body odor equivalent to the pungent aroma of a cheese-fire and, as if all that isn't bad enough; to add to his character, God cursed him with a speech impediment that causes him to shy away from women, and they from him! I doubt seriously if he has ever been laid! Sarge is only about twenty-five but looks like he's seventy-five! He is *by far* the homeliest looking white boy I have *ever* seen!

Although I could never answer the question as to why, for some reason I just took a liking to Sarge. I'm sure this was partially because I felt sorry for him, but more so out of sheer amazement at the man's skill level! *No, no,* not his *working* skills, he had none of those! The skills I'm referring to are his mechanical and driving skills. This son of a gun is a *genius* when it comes to mechanics and I believe he could hot-wire a bicycle! Also, he is *to this day*, the best driver I have *ever* met! Keep in mind that when I say the best, that doesn't mean the safest.

I first met Sarge while we were co-workers employed at a small gas station on the outskirts of town. The company-owned gas station is located on a major state highway just south of the city and is an easy pit-stop for tourist passing through. Sarge and I both worked the midnight shift most of the time except for the occasional afternoon shift where we would fill in a vacation slot. I was only eighteen at the time but my first testament to his skills came the day that he drove an old beat up jalopy into the gas station. I was working afternoon shift that day and had just finished counting money and reading my pumps for the shift change. I was walking to the back of the store to get the large measuring sticks which are used for measuring the fuel level in the holding tanks and also to test for water content. Just as I leaned down to pick up the sticks I heard a series of loud pops, like large firecrackers, coming from somewhere in the parking lot. I dropped the sticks, grabbed a fire extinguisher, and ran to the parking lot where I saw an old car on fire; *smoke was just rolling out the windows*! I immediately started spraying the passenger compartment of the car where I presumed there was a driver and maybe even a passenger. I was taught that if you spray the base of the fire that this would increase the chances of killing the flames at the fuel source and would deprive the fire of any oxygen content. While spraying, I heard muffled noises coming from inside the car and *thought* someone was on fire. Now panicking, I emptied the entire canister into the car, dropped it, and ran back into the store to grab another extinguisher and call the fire department. While dialing 9-1-1, I had my back to the parking lot, and as the phone on the other end started ringing, I slowly turned around and saw Sarge standing outside the car covered in white powder, shaking his fist at me and asking me;

"Wat in *hell* did ye go an' do 'et fer?"

I hung the phone up quickly so as not to alarm the fire department.

"I thought your car was on fire." (*Now chuckling*)

"Hell no 't ain't on far, at's the way hit *always* runs you *idget*!

"Where...in the *hell*...did you get this piece of shit?" (*Now stifling a grin*)

" hit ain't no piece o' shit, 'is rite chair is a racin' car *man!*"

"Well..., I *guess* it has *some* potential. How much did they pay you to take it off their property?" (*Now serious*)

"I paid some old lady eight-hunderd dollars fer it! Ain't she a beauty?"

"Where on earth did you get eight-hundred dollars? *You can't even pay your rent!*"

"Well, actually, the old bag let me pay 'er eighty-dollars down!"

"Sarge, I don't want to hurt your feelings or nothing man, but that thing is a pile of junk and if you *never* pay her another penny, you *still* got ripped off!"

"'at's all-rite, you go 'head an' poke fun at 'er, you jist wait 'til to-mar w'en I come back. I'll *show ye* how to make an old car run, son!"

"Sarge, my little sister's bicycle could outrun this thing!"

"Ye thank so *huh*? I'm a-gonna make ye eat 'em words son, *ye jist wait*!"

"Well, what kind of car is this…, *thing,* anyway?"

"Hit's an ex-FBI car, an AMC Matador!"

"So, it's a *matador, huh*? It looks like it's been in a few rodeos. Did the bulls actually *drive* the car or just *run their horns through it*?"

"Oh, ha, ha, ain't chew a real *funny-man*! Jis *wait…* 'til to-mar!" He said angrily.

" Whatever man! Call me *when* you break down!"

As Sarge got back into his car and drove away mad I thought to myself; "That thing seriously looks like somebody just drove it through a swamp."

I was working afternoon the next day and was standing out near one of the pumps giving full service to a beauty queen with blue eyes, long blonde hair, and a gorgeous body; *seriously*, she was incredible! I was smitten and totally distracted while pumping her gas. The highway in this area is a divided version with two lanes going in either direction with a grassy median between the lanes. Off in the distance I heard this machine coming up the road wide open and as it got closer it sounded like it was gaining RPM and speed. I'm serious, this thing sounded like a Winston Cup series NASCAR qualifying for the Daytona 500! I stopped pumping gas for a minute to see what kind of ride was making all this noise. I was thinking Mach I, Challenger R/T, GTO, Hemi-Charger, Camaro RS/SS; *I am a huge car enthusiast!* What I saw was a moldy white AMC Matador and I *thought* it looked like the one Sarge had limped out of the station in the day before. I started grinning and thought; "*naw*, it *couldn't* be?" As the car drew closer to the station it continued to gain speed and must have been doing a hundred and thirty miles per hour! About a-hundred yards from the station, the car locked all four brakes and went into a full power-slide; all four tires were smoking and the entire car was suffering from a lack of good suspension as the front bumper was nearly touching the ground. As the car drew closer the back end began to drift, the car was now sliding sideways down the highway covering both southbound lanes of traffic. As the driver came into view I could see Sarge behind the wheel, wearing a faceless helmet and safety glasses, and the number "*43*" painted in blue on the passenger door of the old Matador. As he slid past the station I could see that he had the two front windows rolled down and I could hear him screaming "*waaaa-hewwww*" at the top of his lungs! It just so happened that there was an off-duty police officer pumping fuel at one of the self-serve pumps and saw the same thing as I. Awe-stricken, he nervously fumbled around in his truck searching for a radar gun. Before he could set the gun up, Sarge slid all the way past the station, dropped the car into low gear, let off the brakes, and started shredding the rear tires in an effort to get the car moving in another direction, *the road directly behind the gas station*. I would compare it to taking your left hand and reaching over your right shoulder to scratch your left ass-cheek, that's how much of an angle he had to navigate. Somehow, that freak made the turn and was now roasting the tires off the back of the poor Matador trying to get it back up to speed. It was an incredible display of horsepower and driving ability and I could hardly believe my eyes. The blonde was apparently even more impressed with his driving skills than I and seemed turned-on by the show. She even asked who he was! Just as I started to answer, the police officer asked who he was also. I claimed no knowledge of who this person was but couldn't help note that he had put on one *hell* of a driving display.

Unappreciative of my perception, the policeman jumped in his truck and took off after Sarge, the blonde paid for her gas and left, and I went back into the gas station to use the restroom. About five minutes later, right before I exited the restroom, I heard a car doing a burn-out in the parking lot. I walked outside and saw Sarge behind the wheel of the Matador digging holes in the pavement. The rear tires were hissing and little balls of rubber were melting off and sticking to the rear quarter-panels of the car. The car was almost invisible through the cloud of rubber smoke and Sarge was smiling like he'd just won the lottery! I started waving my arms in an effort to get him to stop and Sarge let off for a minute, stuck his leathery face out through the open window, and said;

"How d' ye like me *now*?"

"Damn man, what did you do to this thing?"

"I toad ye I'd show ye how to make one run *dit'n I*?

"OK, you have my attention. I've *never* seen anything like this Sarge; what did you do to it?

"I ain't a-tellin' ye! Hit's a see-crit my daddy told me!"

The next weekend I was working a rainy afternoon shift again and Sarge pulled into the gas station. When he pulled in I was very busy and paid no attention to who was in the car with him. After things slowed down a little I walked over and stuck my head into the car and who should I see in the seat next to him; the beautiful blonde that was in the parking lot the day he put on his driving exhibition. I was stunned that such a beautiful woman would even speak to him, much less get in the car with him! Sarge, sitting behind the wheel, was grinning from ear to ear with his two chipped teeth dangling from his mouth;

"Hey, ye wanna go t' the beach wif us to-mar?"

"No, I'm good Sarge, *thanks anyway*."

"Angie here's got a real purdy sister too 'at's goin' wif us!" *wink-wink*

"Well, maybe I could pull myself away after all then."

"OK, we'll pick ye' up at noon at chore house."

As planned, Sarge, Angie and her sister Rosie showed up at noon the following day for a trip to the beach. I took up a strategic position in the back seat with Rosie and we began carrying on a casual conversation. She was just as hot as her sister and I was equally smitten with her. In the front seat Angie began rubbing Sarge's shoulder and saying real softly, almost purring;

"Sarge, what's the fastest you've ever driven."

Poor Sarge could barely contain himself as I heard the engine rev and felt the old Matador quickly gaining speed.

" 'bout a hund-erd an' fifty!" (*Now drooling snuff*)

"Sarge honey, I wanna go *real* fast, can you speed up some more?"

"Wait 'til I git on the beach road, hit's long and straight!"

God how I wish she hadn't asked *that* question! As soon as we turned onto the beach road I heard the four-barrel kick in and we started gaining speed like an airplane taking off. I love speed as long as I'm in control of the speed and can let off the gas when I want. I do *not* like speed when I'm *not* in control, though, and Sarge must have sensed this;

"Ye wanna make fun of 'er now?"

"No Sarge, I told you man, I'm *definitely* a believer!"

It was a waste of breath as Angie kept priming Sarge to go ever faster;

"I get *really* turned on when you drive fast!" (*purr*)

"Hey Sarge, slow down man, you're scaring Rosie!"

"No he ain't, I like speed too!" Rosie chimed.

By now we were going so fast that the utility poles were clipping past at about one every three seconds.

"Hey Sarge, dead man's curve is right up here man, you'd better slow down."

"*Dead man's?*" Angie asked with great trepidation.

"Yes, appropriately named too. There have been more people killed on this curve than in the number four turn at Daytona!" I shouted, over the roar of the engine.

"OK Sarge, you can slow down now honey."

"*yeee...heeee...*" is all Sarge would say as Angie now started to get a little frightened.

"OK, I was just kidding around about going fast; *please* slow down?"

Sarge now had a death-grip on the steering wheel and all he could hear was that big engine screaming; *he stared ahead like a deer caught in the headlights*! Dead man's curve is a sharp, ninety-degree, left turn with a high bank on the outside. Once you're through the curve, it turns right back into another long stretch of blacktop. The curve was coming up fast and I could see no cars in front of us to slow us down. Rosie started praying and squeezing my neck so hard I thought she was going to cut off my circulation. Not realizing what a complete lunatic Sarge was, Angie had baited him into going as fast as the Matador would possibly go and we were all in Sarge's vortex and at his complete mercy. I could now see the high bank of the curve coming fast but Sarge never let up on the throttle. Rosie and Angie were now yelling for him to slow down. Seeing what he had done with the car previously, I knew he was going to try to navigate this curve running wide open. I said to myself, "well, if this is how I'm checking out I guess I should start praying too!"

"Sarge, *for the love of God man,* slow down!" *I yelled.*

Still no response from him.

"Rosie, lay down in the floor-board, it's our only chance of survival! Sarge *if* I live through this I'm gonna kick the crap out of you man!"

"You shouldn't o' made fun of 'er yisterday!" *he yelled.*

Rosie was now in the floorboard screaming for mercy, Angie was wailing and as white as a ghost. We are now fifty feet from the curve and Sarge hits a little red button on the dash board; the car suddenly lurches forward and the engine gains even more RPM, "Nitrous" I thought to myself! The next thing I know we are in mid-air going off the end of dead-mans curve at about a-hundred and thirty five miles per-hour! The front-end of the Matador was now facing skyward, I got this empty feeling in my stomach like the ones you get on a roller-coaster. All I could see was blue sky and clouds! Everything got deathly quiet, my life flashed before my eyes, and slowly the nose of the car started coming down toward earth again. My neck was now pressed against the inside roof of the car; my hind-end was firmly pressed against the back window, and my knees were on top of the back seat, Rosie was suspended in mid-air between the front and back seat, Angie was upside down in the front seat, Sarge's body was laying across Angie and he was still gripping the wheel. I waited for the sudden impact, but it never came. Finally, the big sedan hit the ground and landed right in the middle of a huge sand-bar, like the ones you might see on a mountain to stop runaway trucks. As soon as we bottomed out, the car began to slow down really fast and we were all still flying around inside the car when we hit the beach! That's right, we landed on the *beach!* I never knew this but there is a small, fifty or so yards in length, sand-road below the curve on dead-mans that leads right onto the beach. The beach here is about a-hundred yards wide and full of small soft dunes. Thank God the sand is several feet deep here and provides plenty of cushion. Usually trucks are the only thing that even attempt to navigate the road as most cars get stuck. Sarge knew this the whole time and only pulled this sick stunt to terrorize all of us. Once the car came to a complete stop, we realized that we were going to live. Angie and Rosie were bleeding from their noses, I cracked a couple of ribs, and Sarge didn't seem to be injured at all! I tried to open the car door but it was jammed real bad, I noticed that the front windshield had spider-webbed, and the hood had buckled. Actually, none of the doors would open and we all ended up crawling out the windows and dropping to the sand. Smoke and steam were boiling from underneath the hood; flames were licking underneath the sides of the car. Eventually, the whole thing caught fire and burned to the ground right there on the beach! I started chasing Sarge down the beach but he was too fast and I was too injured to catch him. I would have drowned him right there in the ocean if I had caught him.

The two girls and I hitched a ride back to town and I didn't see Sarge for a while after that. He didn't show up for work and was eventually "let go". About two weeks later I was working midnight, the town was dead; I was sitting out on the ledge of the sidewalk blaring my Panasonic, when I saw an old Chevy truck pulling into the gas station. The driver appeared to be having trouble driving straight and was slumped over the wheel. As the truck pulled underneath the lights I could see that it was Sarge. He was so drunk he could barely hold his head up and tobacco juice was running down the side of his chin; the smell of alcohol oozing from every pore of his body.

"Sarge, what are you doing man? You're way too drunk to drive!"

Sarge opened the door and fell out onto the pavement; I grabbed him under his shoulders, and drug him into the back room of the gas-station where he laid without stirring for three hours. When he woke up he says;

"Whar 'n hell am I?"

"Sarge, you're at the station man, you're drunk."

"Whar 's my truck?"

"Out front where you left it."

"I took the keys and you're not getting them until you sober up!"

"I jist want my tater chips and my pop."

"Where are they, I'll get 'em."

"*I'll* git 'em!"

"OK, have it your way."

Sarge got up, walked out to the truck, climbed in, locked the door, and fell over onto the seat where he slept for another hour. Convinced he wasn't going anywhere, I started cleaning around the station just to pass the time. I may have had four or five customers during that hour but not much more. I eventually went inside and opened the local paper and began browsing the want-ads. About halfway through the classifieds I heard the truck start. I ran outside and tried to yank open the door but Sarge had it locked. He had evidently hot-wired the truck and was now easing out across the parking lot toward the highway. I ran alongside the truck and tried to yank the door open and stop him but it was too late. He floored it, hit the dip at the end of the parking lot, went airborne, flew across the road, hit the dip on the other side of the road, went airborne again, slammed back down on the paved parking lot, and shot off down a dirt road directly across from the station. All I could see was the headlights of the old truck bouncing up and down as he hit the dips in the road. About forty-five seconds later I heard a loud *ker-wham,* and saw a large pine tree toppling to the ground. Everything got real quiet, I couldn't hear the truck, and uttered outloud *"well, he's dead for sure this time!"* Not sure of what to do next I waited about a minute and a half and here comes Sarge stumbling out of the woods and across the road back to the station. His face was real bloody, he was limping pretty bad, and holding his ribcage. I took him in the back room of the station again and cleaned him up and let him sleep until about a half-hour before shift change. To my surprise, he was uninjured other than some cuts to his face and several large pot-knots on his forehead. I then helped him to my car, drove him to his apartment, and dropped him off. I asked him what happened to the truck and all he said was:

"All I 'member is hittin' a big tree!"

The next night I was working when a police cruiser pulled into the parking lot. The patrolman rolled down his window and asked if I had heard any unusual noises coming from the woods last night. I told him no and asked him why:

"We found an old truck over there wrapped halfway around a pine tree and wondered who it belonged to."

Sarge advised me the next day that the truck had been towed to an impound yard and that the police would never find out who it belonged to because he had bought it from someone using a fake ID, never registered the truck, switched the plates from the Matador to the truck, and threw the tag into the woods after he wrecked.

Sarge eventually would use the same stolen tag on eight different vehicles including a Ford station wagon, a Pinto, a Plymouth Fury, the Matador, the Chevy pick-up he wrecked and an old Army Jeep that he bought for a-hundred bucks. Just as a footnote here; Sarge took the Army Jeep out to the airport, filled the tank with aviation fuel, and outran a new Corvette through the eighth of a mile further encasing his status as a local legend and resident wild-man. I moved to another town shortly after that and never saw Sarge again. The last I heard, he was doing time in the state pen for felony fleeing and eluding of the Florida Highway Patrol across seven counties in two states, Florida and Georgia. The rumor is that they only caught him because he ran out of gas! If only he had been discovered by NASCAR there is no doubt in my mind he would have made millions of dollars and you may never have heard the name Jeff Gordon or Jimmy Johnson. Bobby Allison would have been proud of Sarge for driving a Matador the way he did.

Pags

Ahh, my buddy Pags! Pags is a bit of an eccentric, can't stand crowds, rarely speaks to people he doesn't know, and will fight at the slightest provocation. He also is one of the cheapest people I've ever met. For instance, he hates anything that's motorized or that requires a battery. I went to visit him one day and found him running as fast as he could across the lawn pushing a mower; he never even looked up to see that I was there. He mowed a half acre lawn in about ten minutes. I was laughing when he finally shut the mower down and walked over to my truck huffing and puffing;

"What in the hell are you doing man?"

"Mowing the grass, what the hell does it look like?"

"Obviously! But why are you *running* and mowing?"

"I only had one tank of gas and I didn't want to go to the station just for mower gas!"

"What happened to the rider your Uncle gave you?"

"*I hit a stump with it this morning and bent the blade into an L shape!*"

"Why didn't you just go buy a blade?"

"*Cost too much!*"

"Where did you get *this* mower?"

"*Yard sale!*"

"How much?"

"*They were asking twenty but I offered ten and they took it!*"

"So, what are you gonna do when this one dies?"

"*Cut the grass with a butcher knife I guess! What the hell, you writin' a book?*"

Pags also has a taste for extreme outdoors recreation. I recall the time he went skiing in the mountains, had a few too many, and skied down a slope in zero degree weather wearing only his jeans and ski-boots. He often goes on camping trips into the wilderness and hikes so far into the woods that he knows he can never make it out by dark, thereby forcing him to sleep in an area known for coyotes and bears. He is just one of those salt-of-the-earth people that grow on you after a while.

My first encounter with Pags was the day I was hired into my career position in county corrections. Pags and I were hired the same day and while waiting for our psychological evaluation to determine whether or not we were eligible for employment, I made a snide comment about his hair. Pags is full-blooded Italian and, unbeknownst to me at the time, *short-tempered*. I asked Pags;

"Hey man, what'd you do, *Chia Pet* that head?"

Glaring at me, Pags responded;

"Maybe you should try some on that melon of yours! What'd you do, comb your hair with a hatchet?"

Unable to resist, I responded;

"Looks like you rubbed a little bit of chicken grease in with that too, *huh?*"

"Yep, helps my hair grow, you should try it sometimes, looks like yours needs some help!"

Not bad, I thought. Not one to give up easily, I responded;

"So, how do you keep that spiked look? Stick your head inside the bar-b-q grill and flash fry it or do you prefer the axle-grease method?"

> "I kind of like the grill method myself, it adds to the tan! Speaking of which, where are you from? West Virginia? You must've lived under a tree or a bridge; I'll bet you'd glow in the dark as pale as you are!"

Knowing I was on the ropes now, I had to dig deep into my arsenal of insults and try the knockout punch.

"*Ahh*, so *that's* your secret. *Damn*, here I was thinking you got that tan from the Sicilians!"

> "Say man, where did you get that accent from? The only other time I heard that was from a dude whose Uncle was also his Daddy! You fellas don't still marry your sisters down there do ya?"

Sensing my demise, Pags kept pounding me ...,

"*How come your eyes are so far apart?*"

"Well I..."

"*Are those your real teeth?*"

"Well, actually they...."

"*How come your ears are so funny looking?*"

"When I was a kid I got into a ..."

"*Damn, your head is so big it could be on Mount Rushmore!*"

"I was born with a…"

"*Do you have to take off your shoes to count past ten?*"

"No, actually I'm very good at…"

"*I saw you drive in while ago, who ran into your car?*"

"No one, I bought it from a…"

"*How come you have four different colors of paint on your car? Join the circus or something?*"

All I could do was break down and laugh and from that point on knew I had met a person far superior to me in wit! We were both hired by the county and sent to the corrections academy together. While at the academy I learned that Pags was a United States Marine and had served in Operation Desert Storm as a gunnery Sergeant. During physical training at the academy I also learned what he was made of and quickly discovered that he wasn't really someone that you wanted to piss off. Some fat dude pissed him off and Pags sabotaged his uniform by sewing his pants legs together, filled his boots with shaving cream, and let the air out of his tires! Then, when the fat bastard snored all night, Pags assailed him in his sleep by throwing small firecrackers into his bed. The poor guy was a wreck after that and barely graduated. Pags and I made it through the academy together and graduated as certified corrections officers through the State of Pennsylvania. We returned to the county and were scheduled on the same shift most of the time.

We started hanging out together and would often play basket-<u>brawl</u> with one another for hours after work. Basket-<u>brawl</u> is a convoluted version of Mr. Naismith's game, basket-<u>ball,</u> where two parties box, wrestle, hone their skills in Martial Arts, and train for entry into the Ultimate Fighting Championship, all the while using a basketball as a distraction. During these beating sessions, one is never happy unless one leaves the court with a black eye, broken finger, or maimed in some extraordinary fashion. Most of the times both parties leave with *multiple* injuries, but will never admit to one another that they are even *remotely* injured. To proclaim even the slightest pain or injury is a sign of weakness and *strictly* forbidden! My wife would always complain that if she accidentally brushed up against me too hard that I would swear she had broken a rib or an arm but, in comparison, I'd come home from playing ball with Pags with an eye swollen shut, or hanging out of my head, and barely able to walk, and would never say a word.

Did I mention that we are also the competitive type? Pags and I are *so* competitive that we absolutely hate to lose at anything! We will fight one another right out into the woods over a loose ball, tearing through fences, crashing off trees, destroying hedges, and wrestling on the ground in an all-out war to maintain possession of the ball. <u>Everything</u> between Pags and I has become a challenge to our manhood and has created an atmosphere where there is very little room for error, *if any*. Although he outdoes me <u>most</u> of the time, we both know that even the *slightest* mistake means certain defeat for either of us, as we are close in size, shape, weight, stamina, and disposition.

At some point in our friendship, Pags suggested we weight train together in order for the both of us to stay in optimum physical condition. The nearest weight room at the time was about fifteen miles away and the route included driving on winding two lane roads with little chance to pass one another. The competition started long before we even got off work as we would both jockey for position in order to get to our car first, thus putting us in first place (in front) on the way to the gym. The only possible place to pass one another en-route to the gym is on a half-mile stretch of road called "Wallace Hill". Wallace Hill is one of those places in the road where everyone has been following some slow-poke for miles and knows this is the only place to make their move. Drivers know that if they don't pass you here, they will never get around you until they reach town; another five miles down the road! I have been on this hill many times doing seventy mph, only to have some freak in a car the size of a roller skate blow past me doing eighty! At the time, Pags and I both owned vehicles with wheezy little four-cylinder engines at the time; him a Honda Civic, and me a Nissan four-wheel drive truck.

One day at work we had been discussing how bad Wallace Hill is and Pags went off about some guy in a car the size of a roller skate trying to pass *him* on the hill when he was already doing seventy miles an hour; *all his car would do*. The story sounded familiar. He was so pissed off just talking about it that I thought he was going to have a stroke! We both were scheduled for midnight that night also and had agreed that when we got off work in the morning, we would go down to the gym and work out. As planned, we were on our way to the gym the next morning when I decided to try to go around him on Wallace Hill, *hoping* to piss him off. Knowing that my truck couldn't outrun his car on its best day, I decided to lay back and try to pull a sneak attack on him. It was real foggy that morning too so this aided in my plan to ambush him. My hope was to catch up to him about half-way up the hill and build up enough steam before he saw me. If I could pull this off, I may have a chance of getting around him. So, I laid back about a quarter of a mile and waited until just the right moment to attack. At the most strategic time possible, I floored my truck and slowly began to build momentum. My truck would only do about seventy five miles an hour so I was standing on the pedal when I rounded the curve right before Wallace Hill, now running wide-open and hell-bent for leather. I could barely make out his Honda creeping along at the bottom of the hill and so far it appeared that I was on-target to pull the ambush without a hitch. I was grinning from ear-to-ear! He slowly started climbing the long hill and I was bearing down on him *fast*. I got real excited and now began to laugh out-loud because I had way too much momentum for him to overcome and just knew I was going to make it around him. Just as I pulled in behind him, he looked up and saw me in the rearview. I saw a puff of smoke come out the exhaust of his car as he floored the Civic in an effort to prevent me from passing. As I pulled alongside him I started laughing *hard* and just for good measure, I looked over and flipped him off. He looked over and saw me going around him and laughing and obviously didn't appreciate my humor! So in a very unsportsmanlike manner, he laid on his horn and swerved hard in an effort to block me and *tried* his best to run me off the road. Caught off-guard by his underhandedness, I swerved into the oncoming lanes, started fish-tailing, almost lost control, and lost my momentum; *nearly wrecking*! By the time I regained control, I was doing all of thirty-five, and Pags was gone! Now I was pissed! I almost blew the motor in my truck trying to run him down before he got to the weight room. I had *every* intention of running his ass in the ditch forcefully, *I just couldn't catch him.* In his efforts to elude me, he was darting in and out of traffic, running people off the road, and scattering innocent school-children just waiting for the bus. By the time I got to the parking lot of the weight room, he was outside his vehicle laughing his ass off and pumping his fists in victory! Damn the cheater!

Pags and I are still best of friends but have long stopped trusting one another when it comes to anything competitive. He can still out drink me, outrun me, beat me in basketball, lift heavier weights than I, row a canoe faster, pedal a bike faster, and just about anything else you can imagine. He is just a better all-around athlete than I but I have never, until now, had the good sense to admit it. Most of my stubbornness has subsided and I'm just too damned old to try and keep up with him anymore and really don't want to end up in a wheelchair trying!

The McLaury's
(As told by Michael and Paula Hartsock)

Our year started out with a horrible series of events that just can't be explained in any other way than a test of our faith in God and our will and spirit. I will make my best effort to paint a picture of our year so you get the feel of how this all transpired.

(January)

Paula

"Dylan has been the light of our lives from the day he was born and we have spared no expense in making him happy. He ran our household and we knew no boundaries when it came to coddling over him. Dylan was a huge music fan as are both his parents Mandy and Chris, *particularly* Chris, his father. We bought Dylan his own electric guitar for Christmas that year and he played it constantly while mimicking rock stars that he sees on VH1 and MTV. He even showed potential for having great guitar-fingers and would move his hands around the neck of his little guitar as if he were *really* playing the tune he was listening to! Dylan became ill one evening in January, two weeks after Christmas, after his mother picked him up and returned home with him. Mandy called us and asked if we could take Dylan to the local hospital because he was running a higher than normal fever of 102.7. We have raised six kids of our own and have been to the hospital many, many times over the years and thought this would be just another routine trip of waiting around to find out that nothing was seriously wrong. We took Dylan to the Emergency Room (E.R.) where he was given a shot for the fever and sent back home. Upon our arrival back home Dylan's fever spiked again and became worse than before. He began crying constantly and appeared to be somewhat disoriented. We rushed him back to the hospital again where the doctor took one look at him and immediately put him on an ambulance to Children's Hospital in Knoxville. Upon arrival there Dylan's fever was now approaching *105* and did not appear to be waning. The doctors at Children's took every measure possible to curb his temperature but their efforts were fruitless. Hours later when the head doctor came out of Dylan's room we knew by the look on his face that the news was not good. We braced ourselves but soon found out that we could not possibly prepare for what was about to hit us full-bore in the face. Dylan had contracted a rare case of meningitis and his life could not be saved. Dylan was now on a respirator waiting for his ticket to heaven and there was nothing anyone could possibly do to save him. We were numb and needless to say, devastated! The gut-wrenching news seemed to be unreal and we just couldn't wrap our heads around the idea that his little feet would no longer patter through the house or his warm little smile would never fill our eyes and our hearts again. We have <u>never</u> felt such pain before but somehow we knew that this was not the end for us, *or Dylan*.

Chris and Mandy were now left with the horrible decision of how long to leave him on artificial life-support. How can you *possibly* make the brave decision to remove life-support knowing that you will never be able to hold your only child again? Why does God allow things of this nature to happen and how do you decide which casket will be the best suited for him and how to dress the little fellow for his meeting with The Creator?

Later that evening the doctor came in to ask if Chris and Mandy would consider allowing Dylan to be an organ-donor. He explained that there were two children who needed vital organs that were an exact match for Dylan's age and blood-type; one child needed a heart, the other a kidney. Making Dylan an organ-donor would mean saving the lives of two other children and preventing two other families from going through the pain that Chris and Mandy, and the rest of us, were now forced to endure. Being the awesome people they are, Mandy and Chris made the unselfish decision and agreed to permit the doctors to perform one final surgery on their only child and as a result Dylan's heart and kidneys saved those two other children's lives and restored normalcy to those two families.

After the funeral was over and everyone had gone home we gathered as a family and prayed that God would help us overcome this tragedy and lift us up again from the lowest point we have ever been in our lives. A week after this prayer we received a call from the doctors at Children's with the good news that both surgeries on the organ recipients had went off without a hitch and that Dylan's heart and kidneys will live for many years to come in another child's body. We came to terms with Dylan's short life and realized that we were merely couriers for God's will and that God knew

Dylan would be in no better hands than ours for the journey from inception to the waiting little children whose lives could not have been saved without his organs."

(March)

"Michael (Brook) is a self-employed tree-trimmer by trade and provides his own tools and equipment. We have lived in the same place for the last fifteen years and were previously robbed of an ATV and trailer. Brook keeps all of his tools in his truck for convenience and parks the truck right next to the house. One night in March, someone stole all of his chain-saws, tools, ladders and all of the other equipment necessary for him to make an honest living. Again, we were devastated by loss and weren't sure how we were going to pull out of it. Many family members offered help and Brook eventually bought a used chain-saw and went back to work. Although the loss of Dylan weighed heavily on his mind every day, he still pulled himself together and slowly pulled us out of financial ruin."

(April)

"A close member of the family was arrested and jailed for theft and although the theft wasn't directly related to our property being taken, it was an embarrassment to the family and another spike in the chest of an already suffering unit."

(July)

"We decided as a family that a month-long vacation to the Pacific-Northwest may help ease our pain and aide in escaping the reality-nightmare that we have suffered through so far this year. We have friends and relatives who live near Libby, Montana, and we often travel to this area and camp for weeks at a time. We always lay-over in Pennsylvania where Brook's brother, Phillip, and his wife Colleen, live with their three children. It seems that every time we go to Pennsylvania we have some type of car, or in this case, truck problem. This year was to be no different than the rest. The trip from Tennessee to Pennsylvania is five-hundred and forty miles one-way. About a hundred and fifty miles from our destination, the slave cylinder on the clutch went out which made it almost impossible to change gears in the truck, a 1995 F350, Quad-Cab, diesel, dually. This truck has been our life-blood and never gives us a problem anywhere *except* Pennsylvania! Daniel, our seventeen-year old son, called ahead and let his uncle know that we were going to try and limp the truck into Pennsylvania and that we would call back once we got closer. About ten miles out Daniel called again and advised his uncle to move everything out of the way as we were going to make it OK but couldn't gear the truck down when pulling in the driveway and would have to shut it down as soon as we arrived. Five minutes later the brakes went out, we lost our power steering, and the truck started overheating! We pulled into a Wal-Mart parking lot two miles from our destination and called Phillip. We visited for five days while waiting on the truck to be repaired."

(August)

Michael (Brook)

"After getting the truck repaired, we left for Montana and drove straight through without even the slightest problem; the truck has *never* run better! Upon arrival to Libby we dropped Daniel off at his mother's place and headed for the hills. We camp about twenty miles from town in a remote wilderness area of the Kootenai National Forest. We set up camp that night and awoke the next morning bright and early. Bridgitte (our sixteen year-old daughter) and I cranked up the dirt-bikes and spent the day riding and fishing through the pristine wilderness. We had an absolute blast and caught several native trout that day. We returned to camp that night feeling refreshed and repeated the same thing for the next several days.

We started running low on staples after about a week so early one morning I decided to go back into town and reload for the coming week. Prior to leaving, we hid the ATV and the dirt-bikes, and folded the tent up so no one would steal these items while we were away. We load up in the truck and right away I notice that the truck didn't start the way it normally does. I didn't think too much of it but made a mental note because up to this point I had never noticed this particular issue with the truck. As we drove toward town the truck started running rough so I decided to have it checked out at the local mechanic shop. I was advised that the trucks glow-plugs would need to be replaced. I had the work done the next day, picked up my family, and headed back for camp. On the way, the truck started running rough again and eventually stalled on me. I finally got it re-started, took all the supplies to camp, and stayed for a few days. The truck never really ran right from that point forward and I knew I would have to have it checked again. So, I loaded everyone back into the truck and returned to the mechanic shop.

This time I was advised that pack-rats had gotten into the wiring of the truck and chewed through several wires and several had gotten trapped and died somewhere in the engine compartment. The mechanic refused to work on the truck until I cleaned all of the pack-rats out; the truck smelled like a rotting corpse now! It took us all day but Daniel and I tore every piece of equipment we could out of the truck and found several dead rats in the heater vents, under the dash, inside and underneath the seats, and one way down underneath a fuel rail under the hood. The following day, the mechanic "fixed the truck" and we loaded up again and headed for the hills although Daniel stayed behind this time in order to spend some quality time with his mother who he hadn't seen in over a year. Me, Bridgitte, and Paula were riding toward camp and about five miles out of town I noticed smoke coming from underneath the dash. Within thirty seconds the smoke turned into flames so I hit the brakes and tried to pull to the side of the road. It just so happened that the stretch of road we were on has a mile-long guardrail and there was no way I could get to the berm. About this time, Paula panics and bails out the passenger side of the truck, literally running alongside the truck and screaming bloody murder while still clinging to the door. Bridgitte climbs over the front seat into the back and starts crawling out the back window before I could get the truck stopped. By now the flames are shooting from under the dash and starting to come from underneath the carpet under the front seat. After getting the truck stopped near the guardrail I grabbed my wallet, yanked on my door handle, and it comes off in my hand, *broken*! I had to crawl through the flames to get out the passenger side of the truck; I barely felt the heat and never got burned except for a little electrical spark that fell on my left arm! I had a stash of money hidden in one of the seats of the truck and knew I had to act fast or I would lose it all. I pulled my Buck-knife, cut open the seat, and retrieved my cash. Then I start trying to save my work-tools by pulling them from the burning truck. The truck cab is now fully engulfed in flames and around the curve in the road comes a big Dodge Ram 3500 Diesel with a middle-aged couple inside. Out jumps this huge man with arms the size of fifty-five gallon drums and, without saying a word, he starts ripping chain-saws, ladders, ropes, tools and anything else he can get his giant hands on from the burning truck. He knows we are so far out that there's no way the fire department will get here in time to save anything. He also knows there is no phone service here so as soon as we salvage all we can from the flames, he gets back in his truck and takes off to an area where he *can* get phone service in order to call the police and the fire department. Ten minutes later he returns and assures me the fire department and police are on their way. His wife escorts my wife and daughter over to their truck and places them inside in order to calm them. My truck is nothing now but a smoking, charred, frame and the fire department isn't even here yet.

It was then that I was introduced to Bob McLaury. Bob and his wife Helen are business owners here in Montana. They own several businesses including an apiary, a gift shop, and a landscaping business. By now there are ambulances, fire trucks, deputy sheriff's, water hoses laying everywhere, sirens wailing and lights flashing. My truck was gone, I had no way home, most of my tools were damaged in some way or another, all of my wife and daughters good clothes were lost in the fire, and all of our other property was sitting out in the wilderness with no way for me to retrieve them. I looked over and saw that my wife and daughter were alive and well, I was unscathed, and Daniel was safe at home with his mom. I had an epiphany at this moment and said to myself; "You know what, I LOVE GOD ANYWAY!!!"

After the wrecker came and hauled the remains of my truck away Bob and Helen offered to put us up for the night in their brand new forty foot travel-trailer which was parked next to their home. Having no other choice, we were humbled by their generous offer and accepted. While en-route to Bob and Helen's place I mentioned to Bob that I would need to buy a truck real quick so I could get my belongings out of the woods. My plan was to borrow enough money to buy the truck and pay it off after I got home to Tennessee. Bob advised me that he would retrieve my items from the camp-site with one of *his* trucks and that he had an old truck that he had parked a few years ago that I could use until I found one suitable for over-the-road travel. Later that evening after dinner with Bob and Helen, Bob showed me the old truck he had. It too is an F350 Diesel Quad Cab, just older than mine and a little worse for wear. Bob advised that the motor had been rebuilt about thirty-thousand miles ago and that it should run. After cranking on it for a half an hour it finally started but it ran pretty rough.

Bob and I worked on the truck for several days replacing hoses, belts, exhaust, changing oil, greasing wheel-bearings, and replacing other miscellaneous items; *all at Bob's expense.* After we got the bugs worked out on the truck Bob offered to sell it to me. Not sure how much he would want I told him I may be interested if the price was right. Bob said "Oh, the price *will* be right, don't worry about that!" Over dinner that night Bob *gave* me the truck *free of charge*, even after putting much of his own money into the vehicle, *he gave me the truck*! Paula and I were so moved by these people's generosity that we were at a loss for words and both of us became emotional. As our eyes welled up with tears Bob says; "how's that for a price?"

We lived in the McLaury's trailer for three weeks, ate dinner in their home every night, they even took us *out* for dinner a couple of times, took us canoeing on the Kootenai River, and *gave* us a truck. I found out through conversation that Bob McLaury is a direct descendant of Frank and Tom McLaury, the two brothers gunned down in the "shootout at the OK corral" in Arizona. Over the phone, Phillip pointed out that God had his hand in all of this and that the devil intended to burn my truck to the ground *long before* I reached Libby, Montana, but that God wouldn't let it happen until he placed me in a position where I would meet Bob and Helen and knew that it would work out for me.

We said a tearful goodbye to the McLaury's and headed for home. That old truck didn't miss a beat until we reached the exit to Phillip and Colleen's home in Pennsylvania. As soon as I let off the gas and hit the exit ramp, my brakes got all mushy and I barely got the truck stopped. I limped into Phillip and Colleen's place again where they had a feast waiting on us. Again Phillip reminded me that the devil had *every* intention of hi-jacking my brakes, perhaps somewhere in North Dakota, but, that God had intervened *again* on my behalf and wouldn't let it happen until I was in a position where it would work out for me, and Him!

We talked more that night about how God has always intervened on our behalf when the devil attempts to de-rail our plans and how He most definitely was co-piloting that old truck I had been given for the last two-thousand, five-hundred miles. We made it home safely to Tennessee and I still own that old truck and have no plans to *ever* sell it! It just carries with it too much sentimental value and I know that God drives it around for me every day and that I am *merely* a passenger.

(Closing word by author)

There are times in life that we all suffer such profound loss that the will to carry on ceases to exist anymore. The great light of life may dim to a tiny, single, ray during these trying times. However, a tiny ray of hope, somehow, keeps us hanging on. It sometimes takes decades for us to realize the meaning behind these acts of God, but given time, God heals all wounds through His grace as long as we put our faith in Him.

(1 Peter 1:6,7) – "As gold is purified by passing through fire, so the genuineness of our faith is proved by trials." In short this means; if suffering was limited to sinners, and Christians never suffered, all people would want to be Christians. Not because they really loved God, but just to avoid earthly problems. The fact that Christians suffer too, means that suffering "separates the men from the boys" - it shows who is willing to remain faithful even during the worst of times. (Acts 5:40-42; 1 Cor. 11:19; 1 Peter 4:12)

I know that Mandy and Chris, Brook and Paula, and the rest of the family all believe in God and will somehow come to terms with this tragedy and carry on with their lives.

Freaks, Angels, and other Anomalies

Lucifer

As told in "The Adventurous Life of Reamus Brownloe"

Well, I just turned nine and it seems Miss Kendrick and third grade helped me out a whole lot with my spellin'. I still got a lot o' work t' do though an' I'm tryin' real hard to improve on my writin' too. Miss Cornett is helpin' me a whole lot too and she always say's "cain't never did do nuthin" fer some reason. I guess she don't want nobody in her class to be a quitter.

Uncle Virgil just bought a bunch o' animals and I think he's goin' farm crazy. Everybody it seems has farm animals 'round here. This is more a matter o' survivin' than anything else as cows are used for their fresh milk, butter, beef, and leather for coats and saddles, goats for their milk and cheese as well as their ability to eat just about anything includin' rocks, coal, briars, small trees and other junk (this helps in clearin' large pieces o' mountain land, or "newground") and saves the farmers many days o' back breakin' labor. Horses, Mules, Bulls and Donkeys are used all over the mountains for their strength and unlimited amounts o' energy, they're cheap to feed, require little upkeep, are cheaper to buy than a tractor, and generally are trouble free. Chickens are used for everything includin' fresh eggs, delicious meat, down for pillows, insect control, and even their poop is used as fertilizer in the garden.

We got chickens everywhere because they're cheap and they breed quick. Uncle Virgil has a whole bunch o' chickens around here and sells the eggs to some of our neighbors. All of *our* chickens *and* Uncle Virgil's live with one another and have free run o' the farm for the most part. They sleep in junk cars that were abandoned all over the farm, in the trees, on top o' the outhouse, and anywhere else they want to; just about. In order to maintain a good stock and to avoid in-breeding, Uncle Virgil and Dad will sometimes buy a good stud rooster from another farm. They are always a right picky too and only buy the finest bird they can find within a ten to fifteen mile radius o' home. One o' the farmers up the road sold Virgil a big Dominicker rooster (Dominaker we called 'em) for studdin' purposes. Dominicker's are big ole chickens with small black an' white feathers laid out in a checkerboard pattern, large red eyelids, and beady little dark eyes. This new rooster's eyes are different though and are as red as the devil's, I swear. He weighs purt near thirty pounds, has spurs like hawk bills, and a chest as big as Jim Brown; I believe he can outrun Jesse Owens too. The SOB can fly like a Falcon and I'm not sure but I think the previous owner cross breeded his momma with an Ostrich. He is the biggest baddest, fastest thing walking the farm and *he* knows it.

Well, let me tell *you*, he *is* a stud too and he serves his purpose well. He beats up every animal on the farm and bullies the dogs and cats as well. I looked out the window the other day and seen 'im "beatin' up" an old hen. He jumped on 'er back, shoved 'er face down in the dirt, and pulled every feather out o' the back of 'er neck while she squawked for her life. I told Daddy about it many times an' he jist laughs at me an' say's "well son, ain't much I kin do 'bout it, it's jist natural".

Virgil named the new rooster "Lucifer" 'cause he say's he got the devil in 'im. He walks around with 'is chest bowed out like he owns the place or sump'n and puts down any uprisin' with extreme violence and bloodshed. None o' the other roosters dare challenge 'im either and for the most part are worthless "chickens" now that he's here. Lucifer will attack you without even the slightest warning and dig his spurs into whatever raw flesh he can find. He'll strut around you a few times bock bocking, then, jump straight up in the air and flog the crap out of you; feathers and hair and dirt flyin', you runnin' and screamin' for your life while he's tryin' to rip out your scalp or run you through with a spur, *the blood jist a flowin'!* When Lucifer gits done with ye, ye look like ye jist came home from a long night o' drinkin' and bar fightin'.

Uncle Virgil is Lucifer's whippin' boy 'cause he has to feed all his chickens every day an' is around Lucifer the most. Lucifer wakes Virgil ever mornin' by crawling right up on 'is winder sill and screamin' a bloodcurdlin' rendition of the old rooster classic, *URR...ur-URT-URRRRR.* Virgil never has to git *"out o' bed"* 'cause he always gets blown out from Lucifer's screechin' blast and lands on the floor with a loud bang; soon as Virgil hits the floor he say's that Lucifer will fly off into the woods and let out 'at devilish scream as 'is huge wings give flight from the scene. Virgil say's that poor Aunt Noodle also gits woke up by all the commotion and, *bless her heart,* is all wild eyed, hair on fire, and lets out a cuss word now and then;

she *never* cusses any other time that I know of. This actually saves Uncle Virgil a lot o' money on coffee as he never needs to drink any when Lucifer is around. Lucifer is real sneaky too and will hide behind, or in, trees, behind the corner of the outhouse, or on the roof o' the house and wait for you in hopes of ambushing you.

Just the other day, Aunt Noodle had jist come back from town from having her hair all done up real nice in a Bouffant style (the honey-bee hive I call it). Not one to miss an opportunity, Lucifer was waitin' on 'er in the apple tree next to the driveway. As soon as Aunt Noodle stepped out o' the car and made her way toward the house, she walked right under Lucifer just as he was dropping some little rays o' black and white sunshine. Lucifer deposited several large drops right dead-center in the top of her bee hive and thay sunk dang near all the way to her scalp. Aunt Noodle turned twenty-seven shades o' red and said "well that stupid old thang, look what he done to my hair". She was absolutely furious and started chunkin' apples at Lucifer as he flapped his wings like an old buzzard and let out that devilish laugh o' his and flew away. I have to admit I laughed out loud about that one!

Lucifer has a take no prisoner attitude during his acts o' terror *including me.* I only weigh about sixty pounds, *if that,* and Lucifer chases me out o' my own yard and I am pretty much terrified of 'im 'cause I have witnessed the end-results of 'is work. There's about thirty-nine crippled chickens, dogs with bad eyes, half-hairless cats, and a bunch o' maimed rabbits runnin' 'round here 'cause o' him; *all of 'em* are lucky to be alive! All the animals scatter when they see 'im comin' 'cause they're so scared of 'im. He got a hold to me more than once with 'em giant spurs and that honkin' beak; the sound of his wings beatin' against my head and his razor sharp talons thrashing my back scared me so bad it caused me to have many nightmares o' being eaten alive by 'im, *peck by peck*! This spring, like every other spring here in the mountains, it's rained almost non-stop for several weeks. I ain't seen the sunshine for a long time and the only break I get from bein' indoors is doing outdoor chores or walkin' back and forth to the road where I catch the school bus. This weekend I woke up and it was beautiful out so I decided to go fishin' up Linefork Creek and had waited for this day for most o' the spring and *all* o' the winter. I got dressed and walked to the back door, opened it, and who should I find laying in wait with that devilish grin on 'is face...?

That's right, *Lucifer!* He stood there for a second glaring at me with that big red eye, danced around a little, let out a wild scream and suddenly charged the door. Back in the house I went so as not to be gored to death! I stood there as mad as a hornet wondering what to do. I got *so* mad I started cryin' as I tried to think of another way to get out o' the house without Lucifer knowin'. After a few minutes I went to check the front door and there he was again givin' me the evil eye and darin' me to come out, somehow he *knew* I would try the front door!

Determined to be outside I waited for what seemed like hours until Lucifer became distracted by a large group o' hens that had wandered into the yard. He had been studdin' around the yard for a while and was between sessions when he took a lunch break and was pluckin' away at some feed-corn in the side yard o' the house. I went into Pink-Panther mode and slipped out the back door virtually crawling on my stomach, my butt *high* in the air. I inched my way closer to the edge o' the house in order to sneak up on Lucifer and get an idea where he was in relation to my position. I could hear 'im talkin' away as he enjoyed his meal o' bugs and Indian corn. I peeked around the corner and he was gone! I scratched my head in wonder at how he had disappeared so quickly. Suddenly, I felt like somethin' was shooting electricity into my butt-cheeks and blowing a train horn in my ear...., LUCIFER *again* had tricked me into thinking he wasn't watchin'! He tried to drive his sharp beek into my spine as he dug his spurs into my behind and flapped his giant wings just to add to the excitement. I fought 'im off by rolling onto my back and swarping at 'im with my cane pole about twenty-seven times until I finally caught 'im square on the head. He ran off behind the house squawking to beat the band and I didn't see 'im 'til late that evenin' when I came back from fishin'.

I caught a few Red-Eye and a couple o' small Sun-Grannies and was on my way up the driveway to show Momma what I had caught so she'd be proud o' me. Wouldn't you know it; Lucifer was standin' right there in the middle o' the driveway waitin' on me, *like it was payback time*! I tried to ignore 'im but every time I moved to one side o' the driveway to go around 'im, he'd move in front o' me and try to block my path. I thought to myself; "enough's enough, I ain't takin' no more crap *from this damn rooster*!" I eased down and picked up the biggest, sharpest, gravel I could find, I figgered if he come at me I could throw my rock at 'im and scare 'im away. The thought then entered my mind that *if* I hit Lucifer *hard enough* that I would scare 'im away in the other direction and I could get past 'im to the house. Ever so gently I laid the cane pole and the fish down and gathered my courage. I had watched a couple o' baseball games on TV at a friend's house one time and 'membered how the pitcher would hike 'is leg up, lean way back, wind up, and eyeball 'is target before he threw the ball. So, in an effort to mock this, I lined myself up with Lucifer, wound up, reared way back, and heaved that gravel with all the strength my little arm could muster. *What a pitch*; just as I released the gravel, Lucifer turned his head to the side. As his Big Red eye glared at me, the gravel wobbled around for a split second as it left my hand and sailed through the air like a boomerang; I thought for a brief second I was gonna miss 'im. Then the big rock trued itself and flew like a Chinese fightin' star, sparklin' in the sunlight and making a whirrin' sound as it flew. The limestone found its mark with a mighty crack o' flesh and bone as it struck Lucifer right in the temple. Lucifer let out a wild scream that scared the bejeezus outta me, then dropped to the ground and began to spin in circles, his huge talons raking up the earth and creating a small dust tornado as he spun. His great wings began to flutter and the momentum spun 'im to back his feet for a split-second, he went slightly airborne, lost his balance, and dropped right back to the earth with a mighty crash as if he'd been struck by lightnin'; his giant body surgin' to and fro as if he were being electrocuted. I stood there in fear and shock as he flipped around for a few more seconds and the mighty demons left 'is body, *and then he lay there…, <u>motionless!</u>*

Overcome with fear *and* joy at the thought o' knocking the big rooster unconscious, I grinned from ear to ear. My heart raced as I eased closer to 'im. That's when I noticed a small amount o' blood oozing from his head where I had struck 'im with the large stone. "Mebbe he's tryin' t' trick me again", I thought. I picked up my cane pole and poked 'im a few times tryin' to get 'im to stir. Then I noticed he wasn't breathing; "*Holy crap*, I kilt 'im! I KILT *LUCIFER*!!" I cried outloud. *Oh no*, Uncle Virgil is gonna kill *me* now! I had to get rid o' the evidence *and quick* as Virgil had gone to town earlier that day and wasn't around. I knew I had better think fast 'cause Virgil never stayed gone for very long.

So, I snatched Lucifer up as best I could by grabbing his huge legs just above the talons, pointing his ass ahead o' me toward the creek, and started draggin' his limp body down the driveway. As I took off runnin', Lucifer's head started bouncin' around in the gravel behind me as his body was so big and heavy I could barely lift 'im. His limp wings began to drag the ground around my sides as I struggled to hold 'im off the ground. I slowly gained speed and his wings began flappin even more as if he were tryin' to fly upside down and ass-backwards every time I took a runnin' step. I ran ever faster, now in short choppy steps as the weight of his body took its toll on me. As I got closer to the creek, I heard a truck slowin' down and I panicked; *it had to be Virgil*. I was really humpin' it now and my legs and back were achin' from the strain. Just as I arrived to the center o' the bridge, here he comes in that shiny green Chevy, a small cigar hangin' from his lips. In a feat o' strength unmatched in human history, I grunted and groaned and swung Lucifer around twice in a giant circle and heaved with all my might and somehow managed to swing 'im up over the railin' o' the bridge. His wings flapped one last time as he crash landed ten feet below with a loud *puu...lew..shh...;* he spun around in the water a couple o' times, and then, *slowly...*, began to float away; a trail o' red foam and crimson feathers swirling around his dead body. No sooner had he hit the water than Virgil eased up on to the bridge and saw me standing there all out o' breath, clutching my side, as white as a ghost, and looking like I just finished the Tour *de France*.

Virgil looked at me and asked

"Well, what'n the worlds wrong wid' jew Reamus?".

Gasping for air, I managed to say;

"nu, nu, nuthin' Uncle Virgil, nu, nuthin".

Virgil looked at me suspiciously and continued on toward the house and never asked me again what the matter was. The next day I saw Virgil out there lookin' around and countin' 'is chickens;

"Reamus, *you seen Lucifer anywhar?"*.

"Nope, shore ain't Uncle Virgil, but I did see a big ol' hawk flyin' 'round yisterdy".

"Aw son, Lucifer can lick *any* hawk in the state; I know they ain't no hawk *stupid enough* to try 'im. I hope a Panther er a Fox got 'im so's I don't have to kill 'at S.O.B. mawself!".

I let Virgil think what he wanted to and couldn't bear to tell 'im that I had slain his stud rooster much as David had slain Goliath in the Bible, *except*, the slaying of Lucifer was an accident. I was glad that Lucifer was dead 'cause he was definitely possessed with the evil spirit and now, *as then*, the meek and humble had risen up out o' fear and desperation and destroyed the high and mighty. Thank God, I wasn't the *only* one who wanted Lucifer dead. Hopefully I'll never have to use God *and* Lucifer in the same sentence again! Please forgive me Lord.

Elijah

We all have a story to tell about how we grew up and some of the details get a little fuzzy especially when we re-tell the stories to our children. That is not the case however in what I'm about to re-tell here. Living in the Deep-South in the early eighties was inherently rough to begin with but evidently I'm a slow learner when it comes to learning valuable lessons. As John Wayne so eloquently and accurately stated; "Life is tough enough, but it's even tougher *if you're stupid*!" I presume that it's needless to point out here that some habits die hard in the Deep-South and some *never* die! The ugliest one that I can think of is racism because of the impact it's had on the millions of human-beings of <u>all</u> races who have been subjected to its vices. At the age of fifteen I had migrated to Florida through a series of events spoken of in my second book "The Adventurous Life of Reamus Brownloe".

While living in Florida during my adolescent years I hung around with a wild bunch of "Redneck" kids and assumed many of their ideas about other races of people including Chinese, Jewish, African-Americans, American-Indians, Arabs, Mexicans, et. al.. Basically the idea among my young constituents was that if you weren't white, you weren't right. I was taught by my mother that God see's no color and that it just isn't right to judge *anyone* because of their race or the tone of their skin. But, like I said, I was a slow learner and somehow forgot all of my teachings the minute I started hanging out with these kids/young adults. Although I had been through pure hell as a kid and had been the *victim* of racism because of *my* skin color, deep down I still knew it was wrong to act and feel this way and to retaliate because of my personal experiences was probably even worse. I was guilty of throwing racial slurs at others, getting into fights over racially motivated statements made by myself or one of my friends, and was cultivating an air of arrogance in relation to my own people, the Germans. I was callous and insensitive toward the feelings of others and somehow had forgotten the Holocaust and the needless killing of millions of innocent people. Somehow I had lost my way and now believe that God knew that if he didn't intervene that I may be lost forever.

My best friend at the time, JJ, and I, had rented an apartment together right out of high-school and were working at a sawmill struggling to pay rent. Most of the time we were dead broke by the time we paid our bills and bought what little food we could afford. But, we somehow always found just enough money to buy a case of beer, a pint of gin, or tickets to a good football game. JJ and I were big rock fans too and had never been to a rock concert. A friend of ours had purchased tickets to the Bob Seger concert that was on tour through Tallahassee and at the last minute his girlfriend dumped him and he just couldn't pull himself together and go alone. He called me up on a Friday night and asked if I may be interested in the tickets. JJ and I purchased the tickets for ten dollars each and scrounged up enough money to put ten dollars worth of gas in my old Plymouth, "Belvedere". Belvedere was an absolute gas-hog and most times you could actually see the needle going down as the speedometer went up. I swear this car would pass everything on the road *except* a gas station!

JJ and I made it to Tallahassee just fine and enjoyed the best concert I have ever had the privilege of attending. We hadn't eaten anything since lunch that day and by the time the concert was over, we were half-starved. After walking the half-mile back to where Belvedere was parked we decided to check our funds and see how much food we could afford. Upon turning our pockets inside-out and coming up with a pitiful five dollars between us, a tough decision had to be made! We were running low on gas as Belvedere had evidently gone on a drinking binge for the trip up and only had 1/16th of a tank of fuel showing on the gauge, about a gallon and a half! Knowing we couldn't possibly make it home on that amount of fuel we tried to guess at approximately how much fuel *would* get us home. We decided that three dollars worth of fuel, about three gallons, would probably do the trick but also knew it would be close. So, we bought three dollars worth of regular unleaded and took the remaining two dollars and bought four Krystal burgers to eat on the ride home, barely enough to settle the rumble in our stomachs. On the ride home we talked about how great the concert had been and what we were gonna do the rest of the weekend. The dash lights on Belvedere were not working so I couldn't tell how much fuel we had left and about ten miles from home, now cruising along at about seventy-five miles per hour, the car started sputtering and I knew what was coming. Sure enough the car died and we were fortunate enough to coast into the edge of a rest area.

Now stranded and broke, we had no other choice but to sleep in the car, wait until daybreak, and hitchhike home. As the night began to cool, a fog crept in from the nearby swamp that was so thick you could barely see through it. We were parked in a spot where the lights from the rest area could hardly be seen. After falling asleep we were awoken several times by passing motorist, the Florida Highway Patrol checked on us, and occasionally the sound of a log truck would startle us. Finally I fell into a deep sleep and was having this dream that I was working on a tobacco plantation and a man with no face was yelling at me to pick faster or he was going to kill me. All I could make out on the person was his curly white hair and the approximate shape of his big round head. For some odd reason he was holding his hands up to the sides of his face as if the sun were too bright for him to see, or, like some folks do when they peer in the window of a dark house. Ever have a dream where you are running, or trying to run, and you can't get your legs to move. Or, they move but not fast enough to run. You feel your heart swell up, fear overcomes you, and you feel helpless? During this part of the dream I heard a deep voice say "ARE YOU BOYS OK?" I remember being so frightened that I couldn't answer. About this time I woke up and saw an old white-haired black man, hands cupped around his face, right up in the window of my car, staring at JJ and me. I tried my damndest to eject myself through the passenger side door without even bothering to try and open it. JJ must have been having a bad dream too because he woke up screaming and swinging wildly trying to fight me off. After punching me in the side of the head several times he caught a glimpse of the old man staring in the window and decided to join me in ripping the passenger-side door off the hinges. Before we rip the door off the old man says;

"It's OK boys I ain't a-gonna hoit ye's none."

JJ and I were now gripping the door handle so hard that I couldn't feel my hand, my head was hurting, and all I could see was this ghostly figure of a man smiling and reassuring us that we were gonna be OK. Slowly we crawled out the door, walked around, and were introduced to Elijah, *just Elijah*, no last name! Elijah looked to be about seventy and was evidently as poor as a snake, his clothes were in tatters and reeked of pipe tobacco, and he was wearing an old brown derby hat. Elijah was driving an old beat-up Toyota that he left running while talking to us. I couldn't see any color at all to the car but in the fog it looked kind of gray. The car smoked like it was on fire as it sat there idling and sounded like it was going to die any minute. The rear window of the car was covered in plastic, the exhaust leaked deadly fumes, and I couldn't see a straight piece of metal on it anywhere. Elijah says to JJ and I:

"You boys need some gas?"

"Well sir, we could use some gas but we don't have any money."

"I don't b'leive I axed you if ye had any money, now did I?"

"No sir."

"I'll be back hyea in a few minutes, you fella's just stay right hyea."

Off into the foggy night he rattled in his old beat-up Toyota and left JJ and I standing there staring at one another. After ten to fifteen minutes he hadn't returned so JJ and I were about to give up and crawl back into the car when we heard the old car pulling in. Elijah stepped out carrying a gallon of gas in an old milk jug. He never said a word, just walked over to the car, pulled a funnel out of his hip pocket, and poured the gallon of gas into Belvedere, saving a splash for the carburetor. After priming the carburetor, Belvedere fired right up. We thanked Elijah and he says:

"Boys, they's been many a good white man that's helped me out of a much worse situation than what you fellers has been in and I ain't *never* forgot it. Now git rollin; and I'll foller ye's to town."

Elijah, true to his word, followed us to town and we never saw him again. Just as fate would have it, we ran out of gas before we got home but coasted, again, right up to the front door!

I believe to this day that Elijah was an Angel sent by God to show me how foolish I had been to pass judgment on a man simply because of the color of his skin. I haven't used a racial slur since. Just out of curiosity I looked up Elijah in the bible and discovered that he was a messenger of God and is only one of two people who never died a *physical* death, being taken up to heaven in a fiery chariot (II Kings 2:1-12). Was it him that night? You decide!

Stroker

Cowboy:

1. One who tends cattle or horses; *especially* a mounted cattle-ranch hand
2. A rodeo performer
3. One having qualities (as recklessness, aggressiveness, or independence) commonly associated with cowboys: such as a reckless driver, a business or businessperson operating in an uncontrolled or unregulated manner.

John Wayne, Roy Rogers, Sam Elliot, Clint Eastwood, Charles Bronson, and many others come to mind when I hear the word "Cowboy". A cowboy, as defined by my good friend Mr. Webster, is a man, or woman in some cases, who does many things to help out around the farm. He's a carpenter, plumber, engineer, electrician, equestrian trainer, blacksmith, tanner, hay baler, tractor driver, car washer, and most importantly, a cattle rustler. When I say cattle rustler, I don't mean a thief of cattle. I 'm referring to a man who saddles up a horse, throws a rope on board, and rounds up cattle that have gone astray. If a man has a good horse, and is an experienced rider, the job can be exhilarating if he knows how to handle the animal and make it perform as he wishes. The other side of the coin, however, can be disastrous.

Growing up on a farm as a young boy raised my sense of awareness in relation to horses. I use the term "horse" loosely here. The horses I grew up around weren't really horses as most folks know them. They were a convoluted mixture of cross-bred jack-asses, mules, Shetland ponies, and wild horses. Farmers in my part of the country didn't really care what breed it was as long as it could pull a turning plow or a discus, drag a log, or pull a coal buggie out of a mine. The wilder the horse, the cheaper the horse, was their slogan as I recall.

Sometime in my twenties I had rented a house way out in the country. A farmer, Mr. Barlow, owned the house and didn't charge me a whole lot for rent and, as a result, we had a decent landlord-tenant relationship. His only request was that if I saw any of his cattle escape that I would agree to help catch them. I remember him asking me,

"Kin you ride a hoss?"

"Oh yeah, I've been ridin' horses all my life." I said in a matter-of-fact tone, just so he'd rent me the place.

Little did I know how that statement would one day come back to bite me in the hind-end! I had become quite comfortable living at the farm for the first several months and really hadn't had any problems with cattle escaping. Occasionally I would come across a cow with a leg stuck in a fence, or something of that nature, but nothing really serious. I had turned in to bed early one night during a bad storm and was awakened by a rude, pounding noise on the front door. Alarmed to be awoken at this time of night, I answered the door to find Mr. Barlow wearing a raincoat and brandishing a large flashlight,

"One o' ma Jersey's got a-loose and I cain't find 'er! I need ye' to saddle up and come hep me!"

"Wha..., but I uh..., where did she...?"

"She's a carryin' too and 'bout ready t' pop!"

"But I'm not sure I remember..."

"When I rented this place to ye, you tole me you could ride a hoss! Now can ye er not? 'cause if'n ye cain't, then your ass is outta here on Monday!"

"Well, my memory is comin' back to me now. I'll be right out."

Now cursing the old man under my breath, I got dressed in my warmest clothes, put on my old work boots, crawled in my truck, and headed for the main house, up over the hill. When I pulled up to the barn, I saw Mr. Barlow tugging on the reins of a very large horse named Stroker. Stroker seemed about as excited as I was about going out in a storm to round up an expecting mother. In that aspect I felt we shared a feeling of brotherhood.

Stroker was a well trained cattle horse that had been in many rodeo competitions over the span of his lifetime. He actually won several, including roping contests, barrel racing, and others. I was rather intimidated by his size and actually feared horses to some degree after I was chased around a barnyard one night, and nearly eaten alive by a mule named Sam. The only horse I had ever ridden up to this point in life was at the county fair on a merry-go-round when I was six! I fell off the damn thing, banged my shoulder up real bad, and got a grapefruit-sized knot on my forehead. I swore I'd never ride a horse again. I knew it was too late to tell the truth now and, with the threat of eviction looming, had to play this out to the hilt.

"OK son, Stroker here's a real smart horse so let him do his thang. You jist get on 'im and he'll do the rest!"

"No sweat man, I got this!" I proclaimed with shallow confidence.

Now comes the point where I knew I should have told the truth about my riding experience. The second I climbed on board, I knew I was in deep trouble. I pulled back on the reins and poked the tips of my boots into Strokers giant ribcage like I had seen Tonto and the Lone Ranger do so many times. Stroker instantly let out a loud whinnie, reared up on his hind legs, and I toppled off his hind-quarters right into a big cow patty! Now feeling inspired by my expertise, Stroker decided this would be a good time to stomp around my head a few times and splatter dung in my face. After doing the war dance around me a couple of times, he then ran back into the barn and wouldn't come out. Mr. Barlow yelled at me, ran into the barn, and promptly returned with Stroker, leading him by the reins again.

"I thought you said ye could ride a hoss!"

"Well, it *has* been a while." I said sheepishly.

"Don't pull back so hard on the reins dumb ass!"

"Sorry."

I reluctantly climbed back up on Stroker, eased into a comfortable position in the saddle, picked up the reins lightly this time, and gave Stroker a light goose in the ribs. Mr. Barlow climbed aboard his mount and we took off in separate directions in search of the pregnant Jersey. The rain had let up by now and the moon shining like a lighthouse beacon through the Georgia pines gave off the impression of a thousand soldiers standing at stiff attention for their commander. Very carefully I guided Stroker through the trees. I could faintly hear a barn owl off in the distance singing an eerie "hoo-hoo" as if to say, "hey man, over here". Stroker paused for a moment, his ears perked up, and he turned his head slightly into the wind, as if to listen to the owl. "Hoo-Hoo" came the call of the wise old owl again. Suddenly, Stroker jolted off into the dark so hard that the momentum laid me flat on my back on his hind quarters, my feet flopping wildly about Stroker's neck as if I were in a rodeo, barely clinging to one of the two reins. Instinctively, I tried to raise myself into an upright position but couldn't. Stroker was now running at full speed through an apple orchard and the low hanging limbs were slapping me in the head, almost knocking me off the horse several times, as I teetered back and forth trying to hang on. As we drew closer to the hooting owl, I heard the faint sound of a cow echoing through the trees. "*ma-won, ma-wa-a-a-an*". Stroker must have heard it too as he instinctively redirected himself based on the sound of the cow. Suddenly, Stroker came to a complete stop. It was as if we had run into a brick wall. As soon as he stopped, I flipped forward like someone was flipping a steak, and did a face plant right on the back of Stroker's neck. My feet then went high over the back of my head, while my face was still planted. Stroker whinnied, shook his neck real hard, and I fell flat on my back into a huge mud-hole, still clinging to the one rein. The cow mooed again, Stroker took off again in the direction of the sound, and drug me about ten more feet before I let go of the rein. I jumped to my feet and ran after him through the moonlit trees, trying to keep up. After running about fifty feet, I saw Stroker up ahead in a clearing, circling a big cow that was lying on the ground. Right next to the cow laid a small calf. It was alive and attempting to get to its feet. The mother, still sore and wallowing in afterbirth, slowly rose to her feet and began licking the small calf, gently nudging it with her nose. The calf laid there a few moments, then, on wobbly legs, slowly rose to its feet also, and stood there shaking. I was overcome with emotion at seeing the power of God in the form of a mother giving life. I thought of my own mother and how she must have felt giving birth to me, not to mention my six siblings. I started yelling for Mr. Barlow but got no answer. In those days, cell phones were the exception and not the rule. So, I waited and waited for what seemed like about an hour. I watched as the mother continued to clean her child and the child responded slowly.

Having no idea where I was, or what to do next, and afraid to leave the calf, I looked at Stroker and asked "Well, *what now* big boy?" Stroker looked me right in the eye and snorted real loud. I thought it a strange snort and asked, "Are you trying to tell me something?" He snorted even louder this time and turned a complete circle, coming back around to look me in the eye again. I felt a strong rush of adrenaline go through my body. I looked Stroker deep in the eye and said firmly, "Home, Stroker!" Stroker reared on his hind legs, pawed the air a couple of times, came back down on all fours, and shot off through the woods, the echo of his hooves beating like thunder. I stood there in wild-eyed amazement and wondered aloud; "Can he really be *that* smart?" I kept my distance from the mother and her calf, and watched in silence as the little calf continued to gain strength and encouragement from her mother. I'll bet you it wasn't fifteen minutes until I heard the sound of hoof beats coming through the woods. Then, I saw the bright beam of Mr. Barlow's flashlight, shimmering and bouncing off the trees as he approached. As Mr. Barlow came into the clearing, I could see he was riding Stroker now and smiling from ear to ear. Stroker walked right up to me as Mr. Barlow dismounted and began tending to the mother and her calf. A tear rolled down my cheek as I ran my hand along Stroker's large neck. I whispered softly in his ear, "Good Boy Stroker, *Good Boy*". Mr. Barlow threw a leather harness around the mother, tied a small rope to the calf, and together we all walked slowly out of the woods and back to the safety of the big barn.

I knew Stroker was really a special animal and I gained a profound respect and love for horses that night. After that, every time I saw Stroker, he would run up to me and wait to be petted. I tried to make the time to talk to him every day and never forgot the experience. I made it a point to keep a few sugar cubes handy just in case I saw him unexpectedly around the farm. I even went to the extent of buying large bags of jumbo-sized jelly beans just to feed him as a token of thanks. Stroker taught me what it felt like to be a *real* cowboy and a hero. I'll never forget it.

Wild Bill

Wild Bill, I'm proud to say, was a neighbor of mine when I lived in Kentucky. Wild Bill was a good man as I recall; funny, worked in a coal mine all his life, never bothered anyone, was good to his wife and kids, and absolutely loved automobiles. His love of automobiles was always a fascination to me. Being a big man, his britches always had a tendency to sag low on his hind-end, thereby exposing his enormous butt-crack. I swear you could have hidden a bicycle in it! The thing that stood out most, to me, about Wild Bill was his uncanny ability to keep the most rag-tag of automobiles running, even under the direst of circumstances. He was an ace mechanic and could fix anything with a roll of duct-tape and a good bit of heavy gauge bailing wire! His favorite car, a 1964 Ford, Falcon, was a real screamer! I believe the car had a hopped-up 289 hi-performance engine, with a close ratio four speed. This little car would practically outrun the headlights! Wild Bill drove it for everything it was worth, too, and never passed on an opportunity to squeal the tires. Wild Bill's only down fall was his drinking. He wrecked approximately forty-nine cars as I remember. Somehow, though, he always walked away uninjured for the most part.

I recall one summer, when I was about seven or eight; the Falcon had been giving Wild Bill some trouble. Every day, something went wrong with the car. One day, the alternator, next day, the battery, day after that, the water pump! Throw in a bad rear-end, tie-rod ends, ball joints, busted shocks, and a leaking gas tank, all in daily secession, and you have one real pissed off country boy! Wild Bill got so frustrated that he almost sold the beloved Falcon down the road to some young kid. I remember him coming home one evening from the mines. He got out of the car, busted a couple of lights out with a tire iron, kicked in the fender, stomped around on one leg for a minute, then sat down next to the car with his head in his hands,

"What the hell am I gonna do now?"

"I don't know sir, what's wrong with it?" (I asked)

"I drug the tailpipe off crossin' a warsh-out up on the mountain!"

"Can't you put it back on?"

"Nope, it's too tore up."

"Why can't you just drive it the way it is?"

"It'll crystallize the valves!"

"What are valves?"

"Mechanical devices inside the engine that let it breathe!"

"Engines breathe?"

"Just as sure as you do boy!"

"Why do engines need to breathe?"

"Son, an internal combustion engine, in its simplest form, ain't nuthin' but a cannon!"

"A cannon?"

"That's what I said boy! A cannon!"

"How in the world is an engine like a cannon?"

"Well, a cannon has a combustion chamber." (*Wild Bill forms a circle with his big greasy hands*) "An engine has the same thing, it's just enclosed. A cannon has gunpowder for fuel, an engine has gasoline for fuel. A cannon has a fuse to light the fuel, an engine has a spark plug. When you light the fuse on the cannon, it ignites the fuel, which causes an explosion, which pushes the cannonball out of the cannon at over two-hundred miles per hour. When you turn the key for your starter, a spark is created by this thing called a coil and points, the spark then travels through a wire to a spark plug which is screwed into the enclosed cylinder, and gasoline gets mixed with the spark inside the enclosed cylinder. This mixture of fuel, compressed air, and spark, causes an explosion which sends the piston, *the engines cannonball*, back down into the cylinder."

"What keeps the piston from going out the bottom of the engine?"

"Connecting rods; come on over here and I'll show you."

Wild Bill had an engine torn apart and lying on the ground that he'd taken out of an old truck. He showed me all the moving parts, how everything worked together, and what kept it from flying apart. I was so fascinated that I thought about it all night that night. The next morning I woke early and found Wild Bill up under his car with nothing but his feet showing. I heard something clanging around like metal on metal and asked,

"What 'cha doin' under there Wild Bill?"

"Puttin' some pipes on."

"What kind of pipes?"

"Straight pipes!"

"Straight pipes? What is that?"

"Same thang as mufflers, except without mufflers!"

"Huh?"

"Crawl under here an' look!"

Slowly, I knelt down and crawled underneath the car. I could barely see anything, for Wild Bill's belly was sticking up like a sand dune. I had crawled in on my stomach and when I reached a position comfortable enough to see what was going on, I looked up and caught the smile of a clown staring right me in the face! After further examination, I saw bright pink flowers, green balloons, and a huge tri-cycle; all etched into the paint of the children's swing set!

"Wild Bill, why you got swing pipes under here?"

"It's the closest thang I could find fer tail pipes!"

"Why didn't you go to NAPA and buy new ones?"

"*Pfft*! I ain't got no two-hunderd dollars to spend, 'at's why!"

Wild Bill had cut up the swing-set with his hack saw, and fashioned a set of straight pipes for his Falcon! I laid there in awe and watched as he tied the pipes to the rear axle of the car with bailing wire. Most cars had the tail-pipe running over the top of the axle. Not Wild Bill's, though. The pipes would have required heating them up in order to bend them. He didn't have anything to heat the pipes with so he just put them on straight, *underneath* the axle. He cut aluminum pie-plates, wrapped them in aluminum foil, and twisted coat-hangers to connect the swing-pipes to the small piece of pipe which dangled from the engine, the exhaust manifold. I thought to myself; "what a genius!" It is unbelievable what a human being can come up with when he has to!

Well, as they say, sometimes it's not a good idea to tempt fate! That night, Wild Bill wrecked his car and totaled it! He had gotten plastered at the local watering hole, was driving home in a bad fog, and ran through a herd of cattle doing about eighty miles per hour. Wild Bill said he has never hit anything that hard before and all he remembers is a cows head coming through his front window. When the tow truck hauled the Falcon home, there wasn't a straight piece of metal on it anywhere. It looked like it hit every tree in Harlan County and then got driven through a swamp and a butcher shop. Wild Bill didn't look much better either. I guarantee you it didn't slow him down any though! The next day, he was out hobbling around on crutches and tearing the good parts off of the car,

"What 'cha gonna do with them parts Wild Bill?"

"Put 'em in 'at Maverick over thar!"

"Will they fit?"

"Well, I reckin' they will! I couldn't rightly put 'em in thar if they didn't; now could I?"

"Well, no; *I guess not?*"

Don't ask me how, but, not only did Wild Bill put the engine from the Falcon in the Maverick; he took a rear axle out of a Chevy pick-up, a front end from a Nova, disc brakes off a Camaro, and a transmission out of a Mustang, and made the whole thing drive down the road like a new car. You couldn't really tell by looking at the thing that it was a hybrid mix of everything Detroit had to offer; the only tell-tale sign being the smiling faces of the clowns sticking out from underneath the rear bumper. Wild Bill was a genius who could have ran Lee Iacocca and John Delorean out of the state of Michigan had he been discovered. There are many, many, undiscovered geniuses living in the mountains and barely make it by the seat of their pants every day because they have to. They say necessity is the mother of invention. I would say more desperation than necessity is what motivated Wild Bill, though. May the Good Lord rest his soul!

You Might Be a Hillbilly If...

Ok, so you've heard all of the "you might be a redneck" jokes from all over the country, including some from my favorite comedians, the gentlemen of The Blue Collar Comedy Tour. But, do you *really* know how to distinguish a "Redneck" from a "Hillbilly"? Being a hillbilly myself, I can tell you this; the strict criterion that must be met to qualify as a hillbilly is much greater than that of a redneck! Redneck's, as viewed in today's society, can live anywhere in America and are a dime a dozen. Hillbillies, true hillbillies, live only in the mountainous areas of America and are as rare as hen's teeth in comparison to the overall redneck population! Let's take a look at the origin of each, and then I'll give you my personal input on the distinguishing characteristics between the two.

"**Redneck**": (Wikipedia)

The earliest printed uses of the word red-neck dates from the 1912-1913 Paint and Cabin Creek's coal miner's strike in southern West Virginia, and from the 1913-1914 Trinidad District coal miner's strike in southern Colorado. It is not known where the term originated. United Mine Workers (UMW) national organizers quite possibly transported "redneck" from one section of the country to the other. Then again, its popularizers may have been agents of the Baldwin-Feltz Detective Agency, an industrial espionage and mine security company headquartered in Bluefield, West Virginia, who worked as company guards and spies in both the West Virginia and the Colorado strikes. What is relatively certain is that the term originated as a negative epithet. Apparently, coal operators, company guards, <u>non-union</u> miners, and strikebreakers were among the first to use the term redneck in a labor context when they derided union miners with the slur. According to industrial folklorist George Korson, non-union miners derisively called strikers "rednecks" in the Appalachian coalfields, while slurring them as "sweaters" in Oklahoma and the southwestern coalfields. It is possible that redneck emerged in strike-ridden coalfields to mean "union miner" independently of its use in the deep-south. Clearly, the best explanation of redneck to mean "union man" is that the word refers to the red handkerchiefs that striking <u>union</u> coal miners in both southern West Virginia, and Southeastern, Kentucky, often wore around their necks or arms as a part of their informal uniform. This symbolized their solidarity during the civil unrest associated with the coal strikes.

The predominant use of the term "Redneck" now seems to infer that anyone labeled with the term must be a racist; hater of all without white skin. This too, at times, is an unfair stereotype. For instance, it would be quite easy to unfairly label a hillbilly as a redneck, and vice versa, based on observations that are similar, but not equal, to the traits of the other. Personally, I see nothing wrong with being proud to be white, no more than it being wrong for a black man to be proud of being black, or any other skin color or race being proud of their genetic lineage and heritage. Problems arise when we cross the line and hate others based on simple observations of the color of their skin, their genetic lineage and heritage, or what they drive or the clothes they wear. Enough about the term redneck, for now.

"Hillbilly" (Wikipedia)

Use of the term outside the Appalachians arose in the years after the American Civil War, when the Appalachian Region became increasingly bypassed by technological and social changes taking place in the rest of the country. Until the Civil War, the Appalachians were not significantly viewed as any different from other rural areas of the country, basically because the rest of the country was unaware of the lifestyles associated with the area. *For more information on the plight of the Appalachian people, read the book "Night Comes to the Cumberland's" by Harry Caudill.*

After the war, as the frontier pushed further west, the Appalachian country retained its frontier character, and the people themselves came to be seen as backward, quick to violence, and inbred in their isolation. The truth here is that inbreeding happened everywhere in the country where communities were isolated, without transportation, often without communication with the outside world, and forced to look within their own communities for suitable partners. This still happens in some religious communities, at times, and it's been rumored that these communities go as far as recruiting males and females, from other communities, to prevent this from occurring. Fueled by news stories of mountain feuds, such as that in the 1880s between the Hatfields and McCoys, the hillbilly stereotype developed in the late 19th and early 20th centuries. The "classic" hillbilly stereotype - the poor, ignorant, feuding family with a huge brood of children tending the family moonshine still - reached its current characterization during the years of the Great Depression when many mountaineers left their homes to find work in other areas of the country. It was during these years that comic strips such as *Lil' Abner,* and films such as *Ma and Pa Kettle,* made the "hillbilly" a common American stereotype. The period of Appalachian out-migration, roughly from the 1930s through the 1950s, saw many mountain residents moving north to the mid-western industrial cities of Chicago, Indianapolis, Cleveland, Akron, and particularly Detroit, where jobs in the automotive industry were plentiful. This movement north became known as the "Hillbilly Highway". The advent of the interstate highway system, radio, and television, brought many previously isolated communities into mainstream United States culture in the 1950s and 1960s. Today, the internet continues to enhance this integration from isolation to mainstream.

In a nutshell, the explanations given above are mere stereotypes, and not actual representations of either "**Rednecks**" or "**Hillbillies**". To distinguish the two, one must delve deep into the particular lifestyles of each and bear witness to the two in action. I have seen both and here are some of my definitions, observations, and anecdotes'.

You might be a Hillbilly if...

- You think a dial-up internet connection is making love over the phone to someone in another state

- You have to climb the nearest tree to get cell-phone service from your home

- You own a pair of "creek shoes"

- You know what "creek shoes" are

- You still rent books from a Bookmobile

- You've ever broken your fingers in a wringer-type washer

- You still wash your vehicle in the creek with a mop

- You paint your car every year with a paint-brush and house paint

- Your car burns more oil than gas

- You hacked up the children's swing-set to put dual exhaust on your truck

- You change engines more than cars

- You grow more food than you buy

- You've been injured while attempting to ride a mule

- Wood and coal are <u>still</u> your primary sources of heating fuel

- Goats mow your grass

- You *prefer* an antenna over satellite television

- You use clean trash bags as luggage containers

- You <u>never</u> turn a hungry stranger away from your door

- You insist that visitors always eat before they leave! If they don't, you feel insulted!

- You <u>always</u> pick up hitch-hikers

- You would die, *or kill*, for your friends

- Your sister/s can fight as good as, *or better* than, you

- You've ever used a hot-water heater as a chicken incubator

- You recognize that a good pair of boots is a luxury item

- You <u>never</u> tell a friend no when he or she needs help

- You still say grace over dinner

- Your kid's homeroom class still recites "The Pledge of Allegiance"

- You go to church faithfully <u>every week</u>

- You *try* to live by the ten commandments

- You save more money than you spend

- You can make better liquor than you can buy

- Moonshine is STILL (*no pun intended*) your drug of choice

- You have never sold any vehicle you ever bought because you always drive them until they drop!

- You've been charged a "value added" tax because of all the worn-out vehicles on your property!

- You have all the junk vehicles removed and your property value goes down!

- You're better at catching fish with your hands than with a fishing pole

- You *occasionally* shoot fish (*Beats the hell out of starving*)

- You are happy because your thirteen year old is still in school and can spell, write, and read better than you. (*Education programs need attention in the Appalachians*)

- You collect and sell moss and Ginseng to supplement your income

- Your mother taught you how to shoot a pistol

- You can fly a kite <u>inside</u> your house (leaky windows)

- Your Grandmother wears combat boots and chews Red Man

- You've been shot at for raiding the neighbors garden

- You still believe the Democrats and Republicans are going to help you (Forget about it, they're not!)

- You wait for Ramen noodles to go on sale before you buy them

- You can still catch fish with a cane pole

- All of the tires on your vehicle are a different size, shape, and brand

You might be a "Redneck" if...

- You have more satellite dishes in your yard than there are in space

- You have more furniture in the yard than you do in the living room

- You've driven faster on a snowmobile than you have in a car

- You have a set of smoke-stacks on your S-10 (Only one is functional)

- You've ever gotten a DUI in a boat

- You were arrested and thrown in jail for fighting with your mother over whether or not to eat the pet turkey for Thanksgiving Dinner

- Your primary mode of transportation is a 1977 Lincoln Hearse

- You have air shocks and Super-wide 50's on the Hearse

- You also have Cragars or Keystone Klassics on the Hearse

- You've been knocked out by flying beer cans or liquor bottles during a car wreck

- Your woman's beard, or belly, is bigger than yours

- You name your dogs and/or children after your truck, i.e.- "Dakota", "Sonoma", "Ranger", "Sierra", etc...

- You've stolen a tractor

- You've been injured during a night of cow-tipping

- You have a wood-burning stove in the cab of your truck

- Part of your Fourth of July dinner includes the use of a Sawz-All (reciprocating saw)

- Your homecoming queen wore overalls and was escorted on a Farmall tractor

- You were the driver

- You still wear Rustler jeans and Wrangler shirts!

- You know what "death-bread" is-(bread that you eat after rubbing it on the sodium-chloride coated, and greasy, skin of a still-roasting pig)

- You have Kenworth or Peterbilt mud-flaps on your S-10, Ranger, or Dakota
- You've gotten a DUI on a horse, TWICE!
- The engine on your riding mower is bigger than the engine in your truck!
- You have Super Swamper mud tires on your golf cart
- The *tires* on your truck cost *more* than your truck
- You've been in a fight at the tractor pulls
- You were thrown in jail <u>and convicted</u> for stealing dirt
- You carjacked an Amish Buggie and got your butt whipped by the female driver
- You think Elvis is still alive
- You've ever broken into a trailer specifically to steal a velvet, glow-in-the-dark, poster of Elvis
- You hold the world record in the tobacco spitting contest
- You've participated in the Pennsyl-tucky Olympics (Annual event in Sharon, Pa.)

- You actually won the corn-hole (bean bag) tournament while participating in the Pennsyltucky Olympics

- You *brag* about winning the corn-hole tournament

- Your dogs refuse to take a crap outside because the yard is too dirty!

- You have a Rebel flag covering the back window of your Vega

- You wear a Rebel flag bandana and a wife-beater t-shirt at the same time

- You keep a dog-box in your truck

- You have a gun rack in your rear window

- You own a four-wheel drive Pinto

- You've ever "Road Fished" after your truck broke down on the side of the road while pulling your boat to the lake. Your truck was towed, you stayed with the boat, you got drunk and fished from the boat, and then got a DUI!

- There's a law in your state that makes it illegal to have a fish rodeo! (See Pennsylvania criminal statute 303509-b) Seriously folks, *what the hell is a <u>legal</u> fish rodeo?* Some pot-bellied freak wearing <u>only</u> a pair of cowboy boots, wading the Allegheny River, and trying to lasso a Muskellunge? *Good grief*!

- Your house catches fire and burns to the ground, all your neighbors take advantage of the opportunity and have a weenie roast.

So, as you can see, there are many similarities <u>and differences</u> between a Redneck and a Hillbilly. Unless, that is, you know what to look for. I don't mean to hurt anyone's feelings here but thought this list of anecdotes might help you distinguish between the two.

Good Luck!

A Night to Remember!

Remember the night you turned seventeen? I remember it like it was yesterday! Only because the events of that night were so vivid, and changed my life forever, again! My best friend Keith, and I, had lied to our parents about spending the night with one another. You know the story; right? We tell our parents this so we can hang out all night and do stupid, teenaged, things! That's exactly what we were doing too! The night started out simple enough; take in a movie, sneak a few beers behind the skating rink, hang out with friends, smoke a bunch of cigarettes. I absolutely hate the smell of cigarettes now!

The day before my birthday Keith had rented a motel room for him and his girlfriend. She had lied to her parents too about staying with a friend and watching a movie. Truth is, her and Keith were sneaking around and doing things boys and girls do at that age. Not saying it was right, just saying it was so! After Keith and his girl were through having their fun, we were walking around his neighborhood at about 2:00 am. We weren't really looking for trouble, *per se*, but weren't really trying to avoid it either. The streetlights were all on and we were in clear view of anyone who wanted to see us. As we passed one of the homes on the street, someone opened a window curtain slightly and the light trailing through from the window caught my eye. All I could make out was what looked to be the head of an adult male. As soon as the head observed me looking back, the curtain was quickly drawn shut.

"Hey Keith, did you see that?"

"See what?"

"That dude peeking out the window at us."

"No. Why?"

"Just kind of weird, that's all."

We continued on and soon thought nothing more of it. At the end of the street was a large apartment complex where older folk lived. We were walking through the parking lot and saw this shiny new Cadillac sitting in front of one of the apartments. I said,

"Hey, let's see if the doors are locked."

We walked up and looked inside the car and observed a pack of smokes lying on the seat along with a few cassette tapes. I said,

"Dude, there's a pack of smokes laying on the seat, want one?"

"Is the door unlocked?"

I pulled slightly on the handle and found it to be in the unlocked position. I eased the door open and the dome light came on causing the inside of the car to light up. I looked over the roof of the car at Keith and started to say something when I made an eerie observation; *coming down the street in full view of the streetlights was a man wielding a very large handgun!* The man was running as fast as he could, and as he ran, the silver barrel of the gun flashed under the streetlights like a mighty sword!

"Holy cripes man, *he's got a gun!*"

"Wha...?"

Gun being the operative word here; in unison, Keith and I slammed the doors on the car and took off running in the opposite direction of the gun-wielding sentry. The apartments in the complex were laid out in doubles; several buildings containing two apartments each, separated only by a small strip of grass. Keith and I decided the quickest escape would be to run between the buildings, into the woods directly behind the apartments, and then across the soccer field to freedom. As soon as we cleared the back of the apartments, Keith slipped and fell in the dew covered grass. I thought to myself, "He'll get up and keep running". So, I kept running into the woods and eventually started across the soccer field. Thinking again, "if he catches anybody, he'll catch Keith first!" Then, I heard him coming. This dude was sprinting like Ben Johnson and I could hear his breathing cadence. I kicked in the fear-driven afterburners and thought I was pulling away when I heard a shot ring out from the firearm, immediately followed by the high whistle of a bullet screaming past my left ear. I got really scared at this point and remember the thought entering my mind, "This dude is going to kill me!" Then, another shot rang out, followed immediately by the sound of another bullet whizzing past my head and smacking into a nearby tree. I stopped in my tracks, threw my hands in the air, and turned to face my soon to be killer. In a matter of seconds, I was staring down the business end of the pistol and looking up at a six foot two, two-hundred and twenty pound man. *The strong smell of alcohol filled the air.* I was barely seventeen and just knew I was going to die right there on the soccer field. The man said,

"You are screwing up really bad!"

> "Yes sir, I know. We were just gonna take the cigarettes."

"You really expect me to believe that? Who do you think you're dealing with son?"

> "Sir, I don't know you."

"Well, I'm nobody to play with!"

> "I see that sir!" (My eyes now welling up)

"You think I won't shoot you?"

With that, he shot two more rounds at my feet, causing me to literally jump two feet in the air both times. Then, he stuck the shiny barrel right between my eyes, the silver steel flashing like a moonbeam across a lake. The barrel of the gun continued to flash in the moonlight and with the barrel being so close to my face, it felt like I was staring into a cannon. Looking down the business end of a large caliber sidearm was not in my birthday plans! He pulled the hammer back and said,

"I will *kill you* if I ever see you in this neighborhood again! Do you understand me son?"

I prayed silently to God to intervene and begged openly to the stranger,

> "Sir, please don't kill me? I'm not a bad kid. I'm only seventeen years old and today is my birthday."

"What is your friend's name?

> "Keith."

"Keith who?"

> "I don't know!"

"Don't play with me son!" He said, looking at me sideways.

> "Sir, if you kill me, he will see you and he will tell my Dad. My Dad will definitely find out who you are and <u>if</u> he doesn't kill you, you will go to prison for the rest of your life. *I'm not worth it*! <u>Please</u> just let me go! No one got hurt. We didn't take anything. You will <u>never</u> see me again and I won't breathe a word of this to anyone, *I promise!*" (I said through tears as I waved my hands back and forth across one another.)

"Son, you turn around and run as fast as you can away from this neighborhood and don't ever let me see you here again. Go!"

He waved the gun in the direction I presumed he wanted me to run. I took off running, and praying, as fast as I could across the open field. I waited for more shots to ring out but they never did. I ran all the way back to town where Keith had rented the motel room for himself and his girl. Keith had left the door open. Thank God! I snuck in and closed the door, drew the curtains, and hunkered down until daybreak. I wondered what had happened to Keith the night before. I made my way home the next morning before daybreak and called Keith to ask what happened to him or what he had seen.

"Keith?"

"Phil?"

"Yes."

"What... happened to you? Are you OK?"

"Yes, but no thanks to you! What happened to *you*?"

"I fell down."

"So why didn't you get back up?"

"He was too close!"

"What did you do?"

> "I just rolled behind one of the buildings and laid there until he ran past. He almost stepped on me!"

"He shot at me, four times!"

> "Dude, I know! I heard *four* shots and seriously thought you were dead!"

"He shot twice at my head and twice at my feet!"

> "Did he hit you?"

"Almost! Did you say anything to anybody?"

> "No. I'm glad I didn't now!"

"Good, don't."

> "That dude's an alcoholic and a maniac! His name is Lester!"

"You know him?"

> "Yes, my Dad knows him!"

"Why didn't you say this last night when you saw him peeking out the window?"

> "It didn't register."

"I thought he was going to kill me!"

> "He *could* have killed you!"

"I know, but he didn't! Besides that, we had no business being there in the first place Keith! We could both be dead now just because we lied to our parents! We could have died out there last night and no one would have known why! That's just wrong man!"

"I'm sorry man!"

"It's not your fault Keith. But, I'm *never* stealing another thing man or even thinking about it! In fact, I'm going to look for a job today! I'm not going to spend the rest of my life in jail, or crippled, because of stupidity!"

"I understand man, I'll see you later, Dad just pulled in the driveway."

The very next day, and every day after that for the next week, I begged every business in town for a job. I finally landed one at a gas station. Although I had to lie about my age to get the job, I felt it was a *necessary* lie! Nonetheless, I did get the job. I never missed a day of work either. One day while cleaning the pump hoses, a silver wagon with wood-grain siding pulled into the station. I didn't pay much attention at first but noticed that the man was quite tall. As he finished pumping his gas, he turned toward me and I recognized him immediately. *There in front of me was none other than Lester*! He reached into his pocket to pay me for his fuel; five-dollars as I recall. He handed me a twenty. I counted his change and, trembling, extended my hand toward his. As he reached for his change, I clutched the bills in my hand and wouldn't release. He looked at me and asked,

"What the hell are you doing kid?"

"You don't remember me do you?" I nodded.

"Can't say that I do; should I know you?"

"You did me a favor one night about six months ago."

"What the hell are you talking about kid?"

"Remember one night back in August, you shot at somebody you thought was trying to steal a car?"

The strangest look came over Lester's face and he said,

"Holy crap man, *was that you*? Are you the kid I shot at?"

"Yes I am."

"Wow man, I am *so* sorry! I could have killed you. That was the dumbest thing I've ever done in my life! I was such a drunken fool!"

"Well, you did me a huge favor and probably saved my life because I haven't even thought of breaking the law since then."

"Well, if it makes you feel any better, I'd say we did one another a favor."

"How do you figure that?"

"I sold my gun. I quit drinking the next day and haven't touched a drop since. I started going to AA meetings, and now go to church with my Mother every Sunday!"

"Are you serious?"

"Yes I am! As serious as a heart attack!"

"Why?"

"That night, I went back to my house and trembled the rest of the night. I just knew somebody was going to call the cops because of all the gunshots. Then, my mind began to race and thoughts entered my head of being killed or going to prison!"

"Yeah, me too!"

"I have never been so scared in my life."

"Why would you be scared? You were the one with the gun!"

"I was afraid of myself. I knew that night that if I didn't quit drinking that I would soon be dead or in prison. What you said made me think more than I've ever thought about anything. Until that night, I have gone through most of my adult life as an alcoholic. I have abused women, mistreated my mother, cheated on my wife, and beat my kids! I've just been a hellion all my life and never had any reason to change, *I guess.*" *He says, as he shrugs his shoulders.*

"I don't know what to say."

"What do you say we call it even?"

"Works for me." *I said as I extended my hand.*

"Thanks kid I appreciate you letting me off."

"Man, I'm the one that owes thanks." I then told him my side of the events of that night.

"Well kid, again, I don't know what I was thinking that night. I'm *really* sorry. I hope you can forgive me!"

"I do Lester."

"How do you know my name?"

"Keith told me."

"Who?"

"Keith, the other kid who was with me."

"Keith who?"

"He lives just down the street from you."

"You mean Frank's boy?

"Yep, that's him."

"Holy crap man. Does he know that was me?"

"Yep."

"Wow, I'm glad you didn't call the cops on me. Me and his Dad are good friends."

"And tell them what? That I almost got my ass shot off over a pack of smokes?"

"Good point. Well, I gotta go. Good Luck kid and stay out of trouble."

"No problem sir."

Lester rode off into the sunset and I never saw him again after that day at the station. Which brings me to the point; I believe to this day that God brought me and Lester together that night to help both of us! Lester with his addiction, and me with helping get my moral compass figured out. Like I said in the intro, sometimes the Lord works in ways that are <u>not</u> so mysterious!

Midnight Run

As told in "From the Appalachians to the Alleghenies"

Somewhere, in the dark recesses of the mind, lie these little pockets of adrenaline that are released by such things as rage or mortal fear. For those of you who have experienced the mortal fear end of the spectrum, we probably feel about the same on the subject; not interested in tapping into this any time in the near future, say, at least until the dark figure wearing a cloak and brandishing a sling-blade comes knocking at the door. When tapped, these pockets of adrenaline tweak the mind and body into doing, and seeing, things we never thought imaginable.

At the age of twenty I had finally broken the grasp of Mom's cooking and had moved out on my own, so to speak. I had a decent job, a fast car, and unlimited quantities of testosterone. My place of residence at the time was an old farm house that sat approximately a half mile off the main road, was surrounded by farmland including large pastures and small streams, and was everything a country boy like me could ask for. The property was dotted with very large and very old, Live-Oak trees which at night with the moss dangling from the limbs, bore strong resemblance to skeletal fingers extruding from the tattered edges of a coat sleeve. Compound all of this with low visibility and a farm full of psychotic animals, and you have yourself a recipe for disaster.

The old house didn't have a modern heating system and the main source of heat was a propane heater which had been installed long after the house had been built. I had rented the place from an insurance man/farmer who had a strange love for weird animals. This guy was not your prototypical farmer and his animals were not typical every day farm animals either. These animals were all misfits that the farmer more than likely had rescued from the dog food plant because they were facing certain death for their actions at other farms, or, perhaps they had been rescued from the circus due to their inability to ride a unicycle or drive a tractor; *"who knows"*? They were just downright hideous characters, not only in appearance, but demeanor as well. Every type of animal you could think of had taken up residence here including goats, lambs, horses, chickens, wild pigs, bulls, mules, jackasses, wild cats, stray dogs and any other four-legged, cut-rate parasite that would wander onto the property in search of friendly exile.

The Mayor of the farm was a very large white mule who the farmer had named Sam; I should have picked up on the military acronym used for **S**urface to **A**ir **M**issile as Sam was the most ferocious creature I had ever laid eyes on up to this point in life; I later met a girl who upended Sam in a tight race. That is another story all by itself, trust me. Sam, usually the mastermind of covert operations around the farm, would often organize rallies behind the barn to protest certain indignities imposed on the masses by the farmer. Sam was suspected of tearing down fences, chewing through the side of several buildings, staging forced marches, tipping over water troughs, booby trapping farm equipment, and was in general a well known terrorist. The problem was no one ever actually saw him or caught him in any of these particular acts as he was a very skilled diversionist and manipulated other animals into committing his dastardly deeds.

It was also widespread rumor that Sam suffered from what is commonly known to humans as Bi-Polar disorder. For those unfamiliar with the term, this is a condition which used to be labeled as paranoid schizophrenia. One of the symptoms involves going from mellow and relaxed to enraged and vicious at the drop of a hat. Another disturbing thing about Sam was that he was very cunning and much smarter than the other animals. Sam played the "stupid" card quite often. Sam would lull around and mope like he was sick or something and then when the other animals would least expect it *BAM,* he would suck them into his vacuum before they could escape his wrath. Sam would try to bite them, kick them, run them over, and would scare some of them so bad that neighbors often reported seeing a pig or sheep running flat-out down the road away from the farm.

Humans weren't exempt from his handy-work either. I recall one day a neighbor, Miss McCreechy, had come over to visit the farmer's wife and they were carrying on an extensive conversation while standing near the fence. As they were viewing some daylilies that had bloomed that spring, Sam had moseyed up to greet Miss McCreechy and the farmer's wife. Sam acted all nonchalant, like he was such a nice horse, and let Miss McCreechy pet him and stroke him on the neck. Sure enough, she let her guard down and the minute he realized she wasn't paying attention, he commenced to eating her hat while it was still attached to her head! Sam walked around for three days spitting hair, straw, and scalp out of his mouth and braying from the excitement of knowing that he had claimed another victim. Poor Miss McCreechy looked like she had caught a bad case of the mange.

After bearing witness to Sam's antics a few times, I began to wonder if this was a scam designed by Sam to assist him in maintaining his sick, demented, form of dictatorship. He would have gotten along great with the Taliban or Al Qaeda as a pack mule. He wouldn't have minded a bit carrying shoulder launchers or bombs for enactment of terrorist attacks; he would have really enjoyed it I'm sure. Sam was a burned out, train wreck of an animal and was hell bent on exacting death and destruction on anyone, or anything, he didn't take a liking to.

After leaving home I had taken a full time job at the local gas station and worked very hard to get ahead in life. One night I had turned in early because I had to be up at 5: am for work. I remember it being chilly that night so I had lit the pilot light on the heater located just outside the bedroom in a small hallway. As fate would have it, it was one of those nights you could barely see your hand in front of your face, and, the wind was perfectly still due in part to some strange weather phenomenon that had settled in the mountainous terrain of Appalachia. I was awakened at about 3: am by the unmistakable odor of sulfur. I knew I had eaten too much chili the night before but had no idea... Then I realized, *it had to be propane.* The house was engulfed in a cloud of gas and had it not been for the sulfur in the propane I may never have awoken and been here to tell the story. I quickly turned off the pilot light and began to search for the source of the odor. A good friend of mine, Reamus, who wasn't exactly the sharpest tool in the shed, had spent the night and had been awakened by the same odor and attempted to blame me, *go figure.* After I explained what the smell was, Reamus pulled a lighter from his pocket and offered to help find the source of the smell. After the shouting died down I told him to put the lighter back in his pocket before I killed him with my bare hands. Out of fear the house would explode from the slightest spark from anything, I immediately ordered my former friend to shut off the power at the fuse box.

We soon located and identified the source of the leak as a 150 gallon propane tank which I had filled the week prior. The tank was spewing propane like old faithful, the valve had frozen open, and there was quite literally a cloud of propane engulfing the house. Reamus once again exposed his lack of intelligence by offering to start the car and let it run for a few minutes at a time, spend the night in the car, and have the leak fixed in the morning. Once again I flipped out and began cursing him at the very thought of starting the car and blowing the house to bits. We finally extinguished all possible sources of ignition and got safely away from the house.

My next concern was getting the gas turned off so I didn't lose all of my personal belongings including my favorite car, a Dodge Challenger. I suggested we walk through the pasture over to the landlord's house and see if we could get the gas company to come out and turn off the gas. Reamus was afraid of the dark but had a particular hankering for bombs and fireworks, go figure. He wanted to stay behind in order to watch the whole spectacle if it did in fact explode.

So, alone in the dark, I ventured out toward the landlords house. The landlord lived about 1/2 mile behind the rental property and up over a small knoll. There was an ancient tractor trail that ran along the fence line leading directly to the big farm house the landlord shared with his wife. I inched my way along, stumbling in the uneven ruts of the trail caused by the monstrous tires of the old Farmall.

As I approached the landlords house I could barely make out the ruts on the trail and could see silhouettes of barns and stables and fences and what appeared to be a few cattle bedded down for the night. The only thing on my mind at that particular time was getting help before my house blew up. In my haste I had made a crucial error in judgment that was far more dangerous to my physical, and mental, well-being than the house exploding. As I neared the stables I inched closer to the fence line and began to use the fence for a guide. I cleared the edge of the first stable and...
...HEEEEEEEEE AWNNNNNKKK--EEE-HEE, EEE-HAWWNNNNNK........

The stench of hot, stinky, *Ass* breath and a train horn will make you do things you <u>never</u> thought possible; I was suspended in mid air, paralyzed momentarily, and believe to this day I had a mild heart attack, a seizure, and a bowel movement all in unison. I woke to the smell of burning shoe rubber, running in place on my knees. I began clawing large chunks of sod into my hands in an effort to escape. The finest dung spreader in the world could not have exceeded the amount of material I was moving! I dug a small crater before gaining enough traction to actually move.

By this time, all of the peasants had panicked and joined the chaos, stampeding all around me in an effort to save their own hide. Unfortunately they were stampeding in the opposite direction that I was headed and before I knew it, I got sucked into their vortex. I was not keeping up very well and had visions of being the weak lamb left behind for the kill. So, I felt it would probably be in my best interest to join the stampede while I still had all of my parts. I hitched a ride on the first thing smoking which I later discovered to be a very scared, and unappreciative, Billy-Goat named "Psycho", *just my luck*! As the stampede gained momentum Psycho and I became separated from the pack. Sam, seeking the weak like a giant white T-Rex, saw his chance and came running up behind the two of us kicking his legs in the air, braying at the top of his lungs, gnashing his teeth, and trying to convince the goat it was in his best interest to cut me loose. I would have no part of the conspiracy and clutched that goat as if I were hanging to the side of a high cliff overlooking a rocky canyon. The goat decided to move to the inside rail of the fence in an effort to shake Sam and escape the March of Death. By the time we blew past Reamus, I was clinging to the side of the goat and skip-hopping off the fence rails in an effort to regain my seat on the Terror Train. Reamus evidently thought I was just showing off as I observed him cheering loudly and pumping his fists in the air as we blew by.

Meanwhile, the stampede ran out of steam and all the peasants became mere spectators as Sam continued his hot pursuit of me and Psycho. We finally came full circle around the barnyard and began to approach the farmer's house. I saw my opportunity to eject so I let go of Psycho as he shot off into the dark with Sam still closing fast. I hit the ground as if I were running downhill wide open; arms flailing like a windmill, my head way out in front of the rest of my body like I had just jumped from the back of a motorcycle. Before I could get completely stopped I damn near cleaned off the front porch of the house before getting twisted up around a rocking chair. I was so terrified I could hardly breathe, much less speak, my hair was fried, and I must have looked like something from Night of the Living Dead. The poor farmer, unaware of the gas leak or who was tearing down his porch, answered the door wearing nothing but a large bore shotgun. After he realized who I was and heard Sam braying and trying to eat the goat, he started laughing so hard I thought he was going to share the medical phenomenon I had experienced. All he could utter was "He *almost* gotchey, ditn'e boy?"

After I explained what was going on he got dressed and together we drove back down to the rental as I had outright refused to walk through the field again. The farmer poured hot water over the valve and freed it up enough to close it before all of the gas leaked out. I continued to live at the farm for a few years after that and never had any more run-ins with Sam as I knew to never go outside in the dark again. I knew and accepted my subservient position and Sam knew *I knew* my place at the farm. Sam would actually come by every so often and give me a random braying just as a reminder of that Midnight Run we had shared together and, moreover, to keep me in check; *bastard*! In return of this favor, I would set off a pack of firecrackers or an M-80 under his ass when he least expected it. This would send Sam shooting off into the woods bouncing off trees or a large stone until he would finally realize it was just payback time.

I attempted to seek therapy for Post Traumatic Stress Disorder for several months following this incident but no one, except the farmer and the peasants, would believe my story so I just dealt with it in my own way. Unfortunately, they don't make medicine strong enough to deal with such trauma and neither I, Sam, nor Reamus, can afford to pay for therapy out of our own pocket.

The Last One Picked

Something about being born into poverty lends itself to the idea that maybe you haven't been given a fair shake and that we aren't all born equal as some people think. My thought is this; everyone is NOT born equal. In God's eyes, yes! In the eyes of other human beings, absolutely not! You can't convince me that someone born in the horrible poverty that encompasses the bigger part of the Southern Appalachians has the same chance here on Earth as a kid does growing up in the ritzy neighborhoods of the Florida Keys. Or, that some kid living in the inner-city slums of Chicago or Philadelphia has the same chances as a kid growing up in the ritzy section of Beverly Hills. Let me ask you this; have *you* ever felt inadequate to the point that you felt unworthy? Were you *ever* the last one picked for the baseball team or a pick-up game of basketball? Were you ever bullied because you were small, or skinny, or overweight, or had bad hair, or just didn't fit in with any social group or click? Have you ever been made to feel that you weren't good enough for *anything*? How did this make you feel? Have you *ever* experienced any of these feelings? If not, let me tell you, it's not a comforting thought when you're a kid.

Growing up in a poor, isolated, section of the Appalachians was difficult enough in itself. Although we had a basketball team at the school, we lived too far away for any of us to attend practice, six or seven miles, and couldn't afford the uniforms or the shoes required to be on the team. Organized sports weren't real high on the list of priorities in our family so we just didn't participate. However, we did play our own form of basketball, football, and baseball with other poor kids from around the "neighborhood". We dug baselines out with shovels, used garbage can lids for bases, and pitched from atop a metal washtub surrounded by creek sand. We had a blast doing it too and really didn't care if anyone else thought we were good enough to play organized sports. We also fashioned a basketball court alongside the driveway. My oldest brother, Brook, took an old bicycle rim and nailed it to a piece of plywood. Then, he cut down a tree, nailed the backboard to the tree, dug a hole, planted the mast into the hole, and we had ourselves a basketball goal. Over the years I honed my skills as best I could but never became a skilled player at any sport.

We moved to Cumberland, Kentucky, when I was twelve and I tried out for all the teams but never made even one. I just didn't have the years of coaching that the other kids had or I probably would have had a better chance at making the teams. I was devastated because I really loved baseball in particular. That feeling of rejection and not being good enough to make it onto a team was something I languished over for a good many years. After moving to Pennsylvania in the early nineties, my wife and I adopted three beautiful children; two girls and a boy, all siblings. My son was four at the time and really enjoyed playing t-ball in the backyard with his sisters. So, when spring rolled around, I enrolled him in baseball. Right away, I noticed how quickly he picked up on the game. I learned so much about the intricacies of baseball that first year and enjoyed spending the time with my son so much that I decided to sign up as an assistant coach the following year. Skylar developed into a defensive genius at his level and flourished at team sports. He made the all-star team every year that he played. I was so proud of him. During my fifth year of coaching, I was advised by the team manager that we had drafted two of the "most challenging" players that I had coached yet. I was advised over the phone that these kids would probably be our down fall but that we had to pick them because we picked last and nobody else wanted them.

So, the first day of practice, these kids showed up ready to go. The first was a lanky farm kid, Jeremy, who had never played the game but displayed an eagerness that said "I can do this". The other kid, a red-headed kid named Ronnie, was brought to the field by his mother. Ronnie was about eleven years old and his mother, about sixty. His mother drove a battered looking, long-bed, pickup that sounded, and looked, like it had been driven through a mud bog. Ronnie was so short that the only thing I could see when he arrived that day was his eyeballs and his cap peering at me over the open window of the truck. When Ronnie crawled out of the truck, I noticed that he was pigeon toed, knock-kneed, very smallish, and carried an unkempt appearance. His dirty face, tattered clothing, and sad little eyes, told a story of years of neglect and abuse. He was very shy and would sometimes mumble incoherently when asked a question. He rarely made eye contact when speaking. He shied away from others and hardly spoke to his teammates or showed much interest in being around them. I knew I had my work cut out for me.

At the beginning of each season, just to let all of the players know that I was a real person and not some incorrigible butt-hole hell bent on winning, the first thing I always told my players was this; I will not tolerate *dirt-kickers, flower pickers,* or *window lickers! Dirt kickers,* I explained, are the kids who throw a tantrum every time they don't get their way or they make an error and start kicking sand all over the place in protest. Carry yourselves with respect and you will be respected, I told them! *Flower pickers*, I explained, were the kids standing in the outfield, not paying attention, and picking daisies while the ball is in mid-air directly over their heads. It's OK if you are paying attention, the ball comes your way, you make an effort, and fail. Just keep your head in the game and watch the ball on every crack of the bat! *Window lickers*, I explained for example, is the kid who is playing short stop, there are no outs, has a runner on third who is ten feet off the base, catches a line drive in mid-air, and instead of tagging the runner who is off base, throws the ball to second base after making the catch, thereby giving up an easy out and opening the opportunity for the runner at third to score. Just know what you should do if the ball comes to you!

After warm-ups, I took the two players who were picked last, Ronnie and Jeremy, off to the side and explained to them that I was going to work with them personally as my "project players". Every day, I would coach the two of them in the proper technique of throwing, catching, and running bases; the bare fundamentals. Both kids were eager to learn and seemed to pick up on the concepts of baseball pretty quick. I noticed right away that Ronnie had a great eye for the ball and was very quick despite his size and awkward build. I asked him if he had ever played baseball and he said "one year". Prior to our first scrimmage of the year, I advised all of Ronnie and Jeremy's teammates that it was their responsibility to help these two players become better. Most of the kids made a real effort at helping too.

Ronnie and Jeremy practiced hard and played well during practice but rarely *started* any games. Little League rules insist that all kids play at least two innings and we worked them in as strategically as we could, not being sure of how they would perform under pressure. The progress was quick with both kids but Ronnie soon emerged as the better overall player.

Four games into the season my son, the starting second baseman, while sliding into home plate, got his arm broken by the opposing team's catcher. Ronnie was my back-up second baseman! Ronnie put on this big smile, walked out onto the field, slapped his hand into his glove several times, and played like a little Roberto Alomar. *I couldn't believe it*! He was all over the field making catches that were way over his short little head, diving for balls, making double plays; it was really incredible how this little guy performed! His team mates were cheering him on too and high fived him every time he made a play. He soon became an inspiration to us all and his teammates even watched over him in school to ensure that no one picked on him.

One day just prior to practice, a young man in a newer car brought Ronnie to practice. The young man left nearly as quickly as he had come. I asked Ronnie,

"Hey kid, who brought you to practice today?"

"My wrap-around." He mumbled with his head hung low.

For those of you unfamiliar with the term, this is a counselor, assigned by child services, to assist the psychological development of a child with mental disabilities, also known as "Therapeutic Staff Support" or "TSS". This TSS brought Ronnie to practice every time after that day and I noticed a pattern developing. Ronnie's TSS would pull up, not even get out of the car, and Ronnie would run into the dugout improperly dressed and filthy. This really irritated me but I was reluctant to say anything at first. This was repeated several times over the next couple of weeks. The final straw came after Ronnie was dropped off one day, the TSS left, and Ronnie materialized on the field wearing wet shoes, filthy wet socks, and clothes not fit for a homeless person. His shoes were on the wrong feet, his hair was a mess, and it appeared he had been playing in a mud-hole. *I was furious*! Ronnie's TSS showed up a half an hour before practice was over, Ronnie sprinted to the car, and left without saying a word. I pulled the entire team aside and advised all of them that to let one of their teammates go without proper footwear or clothing was unacceptable. I challenged all of them to do something about it. The next day, The TSS showed up for practice with Ronnie sporting the same clothes as the day before. Then, he just sat there in his car, reading the paper and smoking a cigarette. The minute Ronnie hit the dugout, I practically ran over to the car. I introduced myself and asked the TSS in an obviously angry voice,

"Sir, *what* is your name?"

"Bruce! *Why?*"

"Bruce, I'm coach Hartsock, Ronnie's coach."

"Yeah, *and?*"

"Bruce, if you show up here one more time and Ronnie is not dressed properly, or appears to have been drug through a cesspool, I am personally going to drag you out of that car and whip your ass!"

"Wha..., you can't threaten me!"

"Bruce, Let me make this clear to you, *I just did.* You are stealing from *me* by collecting a paycheck for *allegedly* providing services to this child! Your paycheck is paid out of *my* hard-earned tax-dollars. Now the way I see it is; <u>you</u> *are a thief.* If I saw you stealing money from my wallet, I would assault you! Get it?"

"Yes sir, I think so."

"Good, because I will <u>not</u> be so kind tomorrow!"

I walked back out toward the field and found the entire team in the dugout, all gathered around Ronnie. I heard Ronnie sniffling as if he were crying. I thought everyone was picking on him but quickly realized I was wrong. What I saw brought *me* to tears. There in the dugout was little Ronnie surrounded by all of his new friends. He was now wearing new cleats, a new pair of pants, a new shirt, new baseball socks, and a smile as big and bright as heaven. Someone had even given him a good glove! In my rage, I had failed to observe that the rest of the kids on the team had all brought something to practice for Ronnie. In all of my years of coaching, it was the most touching thing I had ever experienced. Ronnie played like a little madman after that practice. *Every* game, *every* scrimmage, *every* practice, and *every* pitch, he was out there, *literally,* yelling at his teammates to keep their heads in the game, keep their eye on the ball, and SWING batter, SWING! He was an inspiration to all of us and we all grew as people because of him. I have never seen such a swing in self confidence as I saw in that little kid. He inspired me to be a better coach and a better person.

By the end of the season Ronnie had developed into the most improved player in the area league. He would have made the all-star team but he moved away a week from the end of the season and I didn't see him again for several years. I had stopped at the local convenience store to fill my coffee cup prior to work one night. Ronnie rolled up on a bicycle and said'

"Hey coach."

I barely recognized him at first.

"Hey kid, how you doin'?"

"Good coach!" he said smiling

"You still playin' baseball?"

"Not since that year on your team."

"Why not?"

"I didn't like the coaches. They wouldn't let me play like you did."

"Well son, let me tell you, that is their loss! You were one of the best players I ever coached!" I said with pride in my voice and a big smile.

"Thanks coach!" he said as he smiled and rode away.

I never saw Ronnie again after that but it felt good knowing that he recognized me after so long and I knew, *deep down*, that I had made a difference in his life, just as he had mine. Thanks again kid!

Reincarnation

Definition: Rebirth in new bodies or forms of life; a rebirth of a soul in a new human body or animal.

Over the span of my life I have been asked the question; "Do you believe in reincarnation?" I am decidedly not, what some would refer to, as a purple-veined, Bible-thumping, Christian. I do believe in God, though! Although I have always felt that it would be possible for God to do anything He chooses to do, I never really thought reincarnation would be high on God's priority list. My thought was that, "Hey, if you don't get it right the first time, why would He give you another shot at it?" However, I do believe that He has a great sense of humor, gets angry and sad, and becomes vengeful when crossed or disrespected. Listed below are examples of each.

Disrespected: The Titanic. The mightiest ship ever made by man at the time. Unsinkable, right? Never say anything is undoable by an Act of God! That ship was doomed the minute some bonehead *said* the word "*un-sinkable*". Dumb, dumb, dumb!

Humor: Take a look at the duck-billed platypus, by far the funniest looking creature on the planet. God must have gotten bored one day and said, "I'm gonna take a Groundhog, give it feet from a Turtle, put a Ducks bill on it, and give it a Beavers tail. Then, I'm gonna throw it in the river and see if it can swim underwater!" Now that's funny!

Anger: New Orleans! Someone was dumb enough to laugh in the face of God and build a city below sea-level. They thought they could build such a city three feet from the Gulf-of Mexico and build a dirt-dam around it to keep hurricane force tidal waves out!

Since then, they have celebrated open lewdness, used every drug known to man for the last three-hundred years, made their own rules, and defied Gods laws. They must have thought that somehow through all of this; God would be OK with it! Wrong! *Hello Katrina*!

All of this small-talk leads me to the topic of reincarnation. I really didn't believe in reincarnation until after 9-11. I was watching CNN the day after the United States sent our entire military arsenal in to bomb Afghanistan. The television newscaster depicted an awful scene of the people of Kabul, Afghanistan's capital, departing the city in a mass exodus in order to escape the bombs being dropped by our warplanes. The videographer captured the perfect scene to depict the hysteria that naturally accompanied the exodus. In the scene, the sounds of the anger and frustration of the Taliban warriors waving their sticks at our warplanes could be heard and seen. The scared looks on the faces of the children and the long lines of backed-up traffic rounded out the perfect clip. What CNN unintentionally planted *in my mind* that day was yet to come.

After seeing the same scene repeated over and over, it finally hit me. In *every* scene, no matter the location, was this; the clop-clop-clop of the two-hundred pound, overburdened, jack-ass. Invariably the jack asses were loaded to the gills with an entire house full of belongings, household goods, tables and chairs, rugs of various color, children peeking out from the rubbish, weapons, and many other items. Also, invariably, there was some poor Arab beating this jackass with a stick, *trying* to get the poor bastard to move a little quicker before he got hit with a bomb or an errant missile strike. For a brief moment, I felt sorry for the poor little animals and thought "How could anyone be so cruel as to place this critter on Earth, make him inherently small, make him very strong, and very dumb?" Add to this, he has no way to communicate other than the occasional *"Haawwwnk!"* I quickly changed the channel and came across a local news story about a child-molester being sentenced to house arrest for his actions against a three year old girl! I was so angry at this that I changed the station yet again only to see some televangelist asking for money and talking about the subject of reincarnation.

It was then that my epiphany struck; ALL of these jackasses *must be* reincarnated child-molesters, rapists, animal abusers, murderers, televangelist who have ripped off the innocent, and maybe even a few "White Collar" thieves from Wall Street! What better way to punish someone who has committed such crimes against humanity? There really is a God, I began to muse!

As justification for my thoughts, I thought of the archangel, Lucifer. How God kicked him out of Heaven and reincarnated him as a snake. *I rest my case!* Can I get an "Amen"?

Virgil Lee

Cousins, as we all know, can be everything from a best friend, to a worst enemy, and everything in between. My cousin Virgil Lee, yes I'm using his real name, was one of those kids that everybody thought was the perfect kid! He was too. That is, on the surface. When we were kids, I learned over a period of time that my cousin was a great diversionist, and had few limitations on the extent he would go to in order to put the screws to someone else. His treachery, almost always, came at my expense. Now don't get me wrong here, Virgil Lee *was* a great kid but, he used his quiet demeanor as a disguise for the dark side that made him a threat to almost anyone of whom he could somehow stick it to. I, unbelievably, was totally unaware of his shenanigans at the time. Virgil Lee is two years older than I and a bit smarter, obviously!

I recall one sweltering summer day when all the kids from the neighborhood, or better yet, "neck of the woods", decided we had had enough of the heat. We all decided to go swimming way up Clover Lick creek. The creek was quite polluted but we didn't care, at the time, due to the heat. It was so hot that day that you could have presented us with a concrete tub full of cold sewer and we would have jumped in it head first. Well, anyway, we all loaded up in Uncle Virgil's truck and headed out to the swimming hole. Everybody was hanging out of the back of the truck like a pack of migrant farm workers; throwing stones at road signs, calling people names, and passing gas on one another; pretty much acting like the vigilantes that we were. Upon arriving to the swimming hole we bailed out of the truck like a bunch of rats on a sinking ship and made a mad dash to the creek. We dunked one another, had a big water fight, half-drowned one another, ripped a few small trees from the nearby creek bank, and pretty much were wreaking havoc.

I had been in the water for over an hour and after getting nearly drowned in a water-fight, decided to get out of the water and eat some huge, fresh, ripe, blackberries, which were in close proximity to the creek bank. I meandered up to the bushes and began eating away like a starving mule. I was so enjoying the luscious fresh fruit. I was stuffing my face with giant berries that were so big and sweet, and just bursting with juice. I began to thank God out loud for allowing me the privilege of being the first to discover this abundance of His love. I just couldn't believe that no one else had discovered these prior to now as they were almost in plain view, just behind some bushes that protruded out in to the water. I gorged myself until I was practically bursting at the seams and could barely walk, blackberry stains running all down my face, all over my hands, and on my belly. After getting my fill, feelings of guilt came over me and I decided to share the spoils with someone else. I felt indebted to share and not keep it all to myself. How selfish could one person be? I really didn't want to alert the entire crowd so I eased around the corner and tried to get Virgil Lee's attention, "pssst, pssst", I said a few times and got no response. Then I thought how strange it was that Virgil Lee had just been in that area a few minutes earlier and couldn't believe he had missed these berries. Then I started flailing my arms about in an effort to get Virgil Lees attention. After about twenty seconds, he saw me and threw up his arms as if to ask "What?" I pointed at the berries, laid a finger to my noise hoping he'd be quiet about the whole deal, and motioned with my hand for him to come over. He looked at me, looked at the berries, grinned, and started getting everyone else's attention. Eventually he attracted the attention of everyone in the water, about twenty people. I was like "Crap, now everyone is going to eat them". Things got real quiet, all the water splashing stopped, and they all started coming out of the water toward me. Virgil Lee was wearing a smile like a wave on a slop bucket, and leading the pack like Moses leading the Israelites through the Red Sea. As they approached the bank, they all stopped short about two feet from the bushes, and stood there with mouths agape, as if they were witnessing the Holy Grail. I was thinking; "Man, everybody is gonna be so proud of me for finding these berries!"

"Tee he he" *(snicker)* Phillip, did you eat them berries rite t'air?" He asks, pointing at the bushes.

"Well, yeah, of course I did cousin! Look at them!"

"How did…they…taste?" *(Now snickering more.)*

"Oh man, cousin. They're the best berries I ever had cousin!" *(crowd snickering now)*

"He, he, he. Why would you say that? *(hunk hunk)*"

"cause, they're just so big and juicy!"

"How did they smell?" (he… he… hee…)

"I don't know, like blackberries I guess?"

"Well, them's special berries rite t'air Phillip!"

"Really? I knew there must be something special about 'em! What's special about 'em cousin?"

"They've been fertilized!"

"With what?"

"Yeller stuff!"

"What kind of yeller stuff?"

"*Warm* yeller stuff!"

Virgil Lee started clutching his sides and now appeared to be holding his breath. When he reached the point he couldn't hold it in any longer, he dropped to the ground and began rolling around in the mud, laughing as if he had smoked a big joint of Columbian laughing weed. Seeing this, the crowd joined in, and began laughing with him and pointing at me with their hands over their mouths; all of them shaking their heads. Although I still had no idea why they were laughing, I began to wonder if I was going to suffer the same paralysis as they were as I began to laugh with them. I didn't get it until April Banshaker, angel that she was, said very nicely "Honey, he peed on them berries while ago!"

Now I was pissed! I picked up a handful of rocks and started throwing them as hard as I could at the crowd. Everybody dove under the water but every time they stuck their heads up, I threw another one. They looked like a bunch of Dolphins at Sea World. Virgil Lee *had* gone over and peed on the berries about ten minutes after we got to the swimming hole. He knew how much I loved berries and knew I would eventually find them and eat some of them. I was the laughing stock the rest of the day and especially on the ride home. Once I crawled into the back of the truck, everybody picked on me all the way home about eating the "yellow berries" and started calling me "Berry Boy". This would not be the last of Virgil Lee's antics against me.

Later that year, Uncle Virgil, Virgil Lee's dad, bought Virgil Lee a pellet gun for his birthday. I can understand why Uncle Virgil would buy Virgil Lee a pellet gun, I always wanted one too. And, of course, nothing but the best would do for Virgil Lee. Uncle Virgil bought him the pump-action model. This type of pellet gun was the type that, if you pumped it enough, would kill small animals with a single shot. Also, it did not use the standard BB's. Oh nooo... This thing would only accept large pellets that were designed with a hollow point on each end. As most parents know, a pellet gun leads to a small rifle, and then maybe even a large bore shotgun. Uncle Virgil would later come to realize that mentoring Virgil Lee into a lover of guns was definitely a mistake of grand proportions! This is the same kid who would later gun down several farm animals out of pure anger and revenge. (See "The Adventurous Life of Reamus Brownloe")

The only rule Virgil gave his son was, "Now son, don't shoot any birds and don't shoot anywhere near the house". Virgil Lee took this to mean that he could shoot *anything* and *everything* that wasn't a bird and wasn't near the house! And boy did he ever shoot that pellet gun. He shot cows, chickens, dogs, fish, squirrels, rabbits, the neighbor's cat, mailboxes, passing cars, fat kids on bicycles, and practically anything else that came into the crosshairs of his pellet gun. This kid went absolutely crazy and spared no one or no-thing! Of course when his Dad was around, he would always act like he was safety conscious. He'd point the gun at the ground, make sure the safety was on, and that the pump was in the open position. And, he made damn sure his Dad knew how safety conscious he was,

"Look Dad. I told you I'd be safe with it! Didn't I Dad? Huh, Dad?"

"Yep, you shore did son. "at's the only reason I bought it for you!"

Up behind Virgil's place, on the side of the mountain, is an abandoned coal mine where we always played as kids. The land here had been bulldozed and scraped, dynamited and dredged, many years ago, in order to access the mine entrance, and build a tipple for loading the coal. As kids, we used this as our recreation area. It was out of the way, quiet, no strangers to bother us, and free from being discovered by any branch of law enforcement. And, for the most part, we went unchecked by our parents. We played hide and seek at night, had rock fights, shot at one another with bow and arrows, and engaged in many, staged, fights. The Mountain Scouts, our version of the Boy Scouts, always gathered here when any member received a new weapon, stole their parent's liquor or tobacco product, or had scandalous information to share about the neighbors. The Mountain Scouts had gathered this particular day to check out Virgil Lee's new pellet rifle. We were all, about ten of us, standing around in a giant circle admiring the new addition to our already huge arsenal,

It's purdy hain't it boys?"

"Shore is Virgil Lee!" *Roscoe said*

"Looky here at this pump action."

"Geez, How many times you gonna pump it?"

"'Til I cain't no more!"

"Won't that break it?"

"It's got a warranty!"

"What are you gonna shoot with it?"

"I 'ont know yit. Mebbe Phillip! Wouldn't 'at be funny?"

"Wouldn't be funny to me!" *I said*.

"You better take off runnin' then!"

"What? Are you *seriously* gonna shoot me?"

"Yep, shore am. Now git to runnin'."

"Man, 'at ain't right. What if I don't run?"

"He.., he. Then I'll jist shoot you right here, dum-dum!"

As if the idea of being shot by my own cousin wasn't enough, Virgil Lee was now standing on the barrel of the pellet gun and pushing the pump down with his foot. I really didn't think he would shoot me, I guess. So, like an idiot, I stood there until he could no longer squeeze another pound of air-pressure into the cylinder. He picks the gun up, flips the safety off, points the gun at me, and says, *laughing,*

"Phillip, 'is gone hurt awful bad at close range, you better take off! *Hee, he, he...*"

Now seeing the serious look in his eye, I took off. I got about ten feet and felt the sting of a lead pellet in my butt cheek. I yelped, grabbed my hind-end, and caught another gear before he could get the next pellet in the gun, dust boiling up behind me as I ran. I turned around to see what he was doing and caught a glimpse of the pump action going back and forth, him doubled over and laughing so hard he could hardly squeeze the handle. I darted behind a pine tree, and then another, and another, until I finally got myself out of range of the pellet rifle. I could still hear them smacking off the trees as I ran. I hurt for three days after that and was constantly scratching my butt because of the sizeable lump on my butt-cheek left by the sting of the lead pellet! Every time Virgil Lee saw me, he laughed out loud at the sight of me scratching my butt.

The fourth of July that year, 1976, Virgil Lee was introduced to the most famous of firecrackers, the M-80! For those of you unfamiliar with this item, it is about the equivalent of a quarter-stick of dynamite. Somehow, Virgil Lee had bartered with a kid whose Dad was into fireworks real big and gained possession of about ten of them. He also managed to get bottle rockets, small firecrackers, sparklers, and many other fireworks. Nothing in the neighborhood was safe now. Just for fun, Virgil Lee stuck one down into the gas tank of an abandoned car just to watch the back end of the car jump up off the ground. Then, he stuck one in a mailbox, closed the lid, and blew the mailbox to shreds. He threw two more in the Big-Hole, our fishing and swimming hole, killing about fifteen fish. Evidently, this didn't provide enough entertainment value for him, so, he decided to get a little more creative.

That night, he waited patiently, plotting where and when he would strike next. Lucky me, I had gotten up at about midnight that night to go to the outhouse. At that age, I was pretty much terrified of the dark anyway and needed no further inspiration to be scared. I crept out to the old outhouse, closed the door, dropped my britches and drawers, and sat down to squeeze one out. About halfway through the operation, I heard a fizz, smelled acrid smoke, and saw a sparkle coming from inside the hole of the seat. Thinking it was only a sparkler, I shouted,

"That's real funny Virgil Lee."

Then, I heard that goofy laugh of his,

"*Hee, he, he,* you better git outta there quick Phillip, or you gonna stink real bad!"

"*Huh?*" **Ker-booom**

I felt a large "something" splat me right in the hind-end, I jumped down off the seat, and ran out of the outhouse with my britches and drawers dangling around my ankles. My ears were ringing and I smelled like doo-doo. Both houses emptied to see me standing there in the moonlight, butt-naked, covered in poop, and mad as a hornet. Everybody thought I had set off an M-80 and then fell into the poop tank. Virgil Lee ran off into the woods and couldn't be found until the next day.

Uncle Virgil made Virgil Lee clean the outhouse, apologize to me, and swear to never use fireworks again. To this day, Virgil Lee is one of my favorite cousins, if not *the* favorite. He taught me to be creative, how to overcome adversity, how to deal with stress in a positive way, and never, ever allowed me to get bored! Virgil Lee; I Love You Man!!!

Freaks, Angels, and other Anomalies

- Other books by this author, "From the Appalachians to the Alleghenies", (2009)

- The Adventurous Life of Reamus Brownloe (2010)

- For the latest information on my books, visit me on Facebook at Lineforkpublishing, or, email me at lineforkpublishing@yahoo.com

- Special thanks to Mandy Call and Chris Rodgers, parents of Dylan Rodgers.

- Many thanks to my first cousin, the infamous Virgil Lee Cantrell, for input on several stories.

Copyright, Linefork Publishing, August 2010

This book is the sole property of Phillip Bryan Hartsock, DBA Linefork Publishing. Nothing in this book is to be reproduced, copied, or edited without written permission from Phillip Bryan Hartsock!

All copyright laws apply to this document.

www.ingramcontent.com/pod-product-compliance
Lightning Source LLC
LaVergne TN
LVHW041614070426
835507LV00008B/232